D0187142

365
Ways to
Attract
Good
Luck

Photo © Jason Fell

About the Author

Richard Webster was born and raised in New Zealand. He has been interested in the psychic world since he was nine years old. As a teenager, he became involved in hypnotism and later became a professional stage hypnotist. After school, he worked in the publishing business and purchased a bookstore. The concept of reincarnation played a significant role in his decision to become a past-life specialist. Richard has also taught psychic development classes, which are based on many of his books.

Richard's first book was published in 1972, fulfilling a childhood dream of becoming an author. Richard is now the author of more than fifty books, and he is still writing today. His best-selling books include *Spirit Guides & Angel Guardians* and *Creative Visualization for Beginners*.

Richard has appeared on several radio and TV programs in the United States and abroad including guest spots on *Hard Copy*, WMAQ-TV (Chicago), KTLA-TV (Los Angeles), KSTW-TV (Seattle) and *The Mike and Matty Show* (ABC). He currently resides in New Zealand with his wife and three children. He regularly travels the world to give lectures and workshops and to continue his research.

Richard Webster

365
Ways to
Attract
Good
Luck

Simple Steps to Take Control
of Chance and Improve
Your Fortune

Llewellyn Publications
Woodbury, Minnesota

365 Ways to Attract Good Luck: Simple Steps to Take Control of Chance and Improve Your Future
© 2014 by Richard Webster. All rights reserved. No part of this book may be used or reproduced in any manner whatsoever, including Internet usage, without written permission from Llewellyn Publications, except in the case of brief quotations embodied in critical articles and reviews.

FIRST EDITION
First Printing, 2014

Book design by Bob Gaul
Cover art: Shutterstock/135287159/©Yutilova Elena
            iStockphoto.com/1735753/©kerkla
Cover design by Lisa Novak
Editing by Laura Graves

Llewellyn Publications is a registered trademark of Llewellyn Worldwide Ltd.

Library of Congress Cataloging-in-Publication Data
Webster, Richard, 1946–
  365 ways to attract good luck: simple steps to take control of chance
and improve your fortune/Richard Webster.—First Edition.
     pages cm
  Includes bibliographical references.
  ISBN 978-0-7387-3893-2
1. Fortune. 2. Chance. 3. Success. I. Title. II. Title:
Three hundred sixty-five ways to attract good luck.
  BF1778.W43 2014
  131—dc23

                          2014014772

Llewellyn Worldwide Ltd. does not participate in, endorse, or have any authority or responsibility concerning private business transactions between our authors and the public.

All mail addressed to the author is forwarded but the publisher cannot, unless specifically instructed by the author, give out an address or phone number.

Any Internet references contained in this work are current at publication time, but the publisher cannot guarantee that a specific location will continue to be maintained. Please refer to the publisher's website for links to authors' websites and other sources.

Llewellyn Publications, a Division of Llewellyn Worldwide Ltd.
2143 Wooddale Drive
Woodbury, MN 55125-2989
www.llewellyn.com
Printed in the United States of America

For my good friend
Brett Sloman

Contents

Part Two—Lucky Tools

Chapter Three: Lucky Words and Phrases   61

Chapter Four: Lucky Crystals and Gemstones   67

Chapter Five: Lucky Charms   77

....

Part Three—Luck by Category

....

Chapter Six: Love and Marriage   107

Chapter Seven: Luck in the Home   121

Chapter Eight: Seasons, Days, Months, and Years   133

Part Four—Luck Throughout Culture and History

Introduction:

What Is Luck, and What Can You Do About It?

Luck has been defined as the combination of chance circumstances that bring good or ill into a person's life. If this definition is correct, luck is unpredictable. E. M. Forster (1879–1970), the English novelist, referred to this when he wrote: "There is much good luck in the world, but it is luck. We are none of us safe. We are children, playing or quarrelling on the line." [1]

Over the centuries, many people have tried to explain luck. Some people think the architect of the universe creates the situations in which good or bad luck can occur. Others believe trusting their intuition will bring them good luck. Still others claim there's no such thing as luck, and pure chance is responsible for every instance of good or bad luck. Author Max Gunther wrote: "Luck is the supreme insult to human reason: You can't plan for it, you can't cultivate it, and you can't find anybody to teach it to you. All you can do is hope for it." [2]

I would strongly disagree! We do have influence over our luck, which is reassuring when life can often feel like you're at chance's whim. Although luck doesn't directly govern our lives, it affects nearly everything we do. Consequently, people have tried throughout history to improve their luck by using rituals, lucky charms, positive thinking, philosophies such as feng shui, and divination—techniques we'll be reviewing in this book.

Good Luck

Luck is a mysterious force that seems to operate for good or ill in people's lives. Sir Winston Churchill (1874–1965) was known as "that lucky devil Churchill" because most of the time, events seemed to work out in a way that favored him. In recent years, scientists have started looking at some of these practices to determine if they can help people improve their luck. Lysann Damisch of the University of Cologne became interested in the superstitions of professional athletes such as Michael Jordan, and created a test to see if these practices genuinely gave them more luck. In one experiment, she asked volunteers to bring a lucky charm with them when they took a test. The charms were taken away to be photographed, and half the volunteers received them back before the test began. The people who had their lucky charm with them did better at the test because they felt more confident. Professor Damisch found that even wishing someone "good luck" improved his or her results as it created confidence.[3]

It seems that superstitious practices can increase luck, as they give people more confidence and the illusion of control in stressful situations. Giora Keinan of the University of Tel Aviv found that people knocked on wood more frequently after being asked stress-inducing questions, such as: "Have you ever been involved in a terrible road accident?"[4]

Random chances of fate can create good or bad luck. Winning a lottery is an example of this. Winning a large sum of money when the odds are millions to one against you is certainly an example of luck. This may not necessarily be good luck, either, as statistically two out of every three lottery winners spend or lose their winnings in less than five years.

People often refer to other people's amazing successes as luck, ignoring the fact that talent, hard work, persistence, and other factors were probably more important in achieving success than pure luck. Often, apparent overnight success is the result of many years of hard work that has ultimately paid off with a seemingly lucky result.

Of course, while there are ways you can influence luck, some things can't be changed. Your ancestors and country of birth are obvious examples. In some countries, parents feel luckier if they produce a boy rather than a girl. This is because the boy will grow up and help support the family, whereas a girl will grow up and ultimately help the family she marries into. For this reason, someone born in a first-world country would probably be considered lucky compared to someone born in a third-world country. Someone born to loving parents would be considered luckier than someone born to parents who hated each other. Wealthy parents might be considered luckier than parents who have to struggle to make a living.

However, even in these situations, the opposite might well be true. A child born to wealthy parents who showered him or her with expensive gifts but withheld love is not as lucky as someone with poor parents who constantly demonstrate how much they love their child.

Bad Luck

There is also bad luck. So-called "acts of God" such as earthquakes, tsunamis, and tornados can cause unbelievable devastation and destroy people's lives in a matter of moments. A friend of mine was diagnosed with cancer shortly after he retired, and died just a few months later. He was looking forward to starting a new career as an artist. That's definitely an example of bad luck.

What's Your Opinion of Luck?

Many years ago I met a man who told me he was never lucky. He felt life had conspired against him, and it was a waste of time even trying to get ahead because fate would work against him. I've thought about him often over the years, as I felt it was his thoughts that created his apparent bad luck. I've always been grateful to him. If this chance meeting had not occurred, I may not have become interested in the subject of luck, and this book would never have been written. This probably means that meeting him was lucky for me.

Not surprisingly, there are numerous proverbs that relate to luck. Here are some examples:

+ See a pin and pick it up. All day long you'll have good luck.

+ Bad luck for one man is good luck for another.

+ Speak little of your bad luck, and don't boast about your good luck.

+ Luck knows no limits.

+ Luck favors the bold.

+ Third time lucky.

+ Luck is the idol of the idle.

+ It's better to be born lucky than rich.

+ Don't push your luck.

+ Guests bring good luck with them.

+ Never trust luck alone.

+ Luck never gives, it only lends.

+ Good luck beats early rising.

- He has the luck of the Irish.

- Cowards have no luck.

- Diligence is the mother of good luck.

- Luck sometimes visits a fool, but it never sits down with him.

- You don't need intelligence to have luck, but you need luck to have intelligence.

- Lucky at cards, unlucky at love (this last one is interesting, as it effectively says that if you're lucky in one area of life, you won't necessarily be lucky elsewhere).

No matter what your current beliefs on luck may be, I challenge you to put them aside and test new waters! Try the practices here and watch as you begin attracting good luck. I don't accept that luck is totally random and unpredictable; I believe we create our own luck, good or bad, by the way we live our lives. The primary purpose of this book is to demonstrate the idea and show you how you can improve your own luck. You may not be able to control what happens to you, but you always retain the ability to control your reactions. If you want to become lucky, like that "lucky devil Churchill," it is entirely up to you. With the help of this book, you can create your own good luck. It's never too late.

This book also looks at a variety of different items and rituals people have used over the years to try to improve their luck. These methods work as long as you believe they will. I own a collection of "lucky" objects, and frequently select one to take with me when I particularly want luck on my side. I find it fascinating that I always seem to do better when I'm carrying a lucky charm than when I don't. I don't believe that good luck is imbued in the object, though. I'm luckier on these occasions because the charm makes me think of luck, and reminds me how lucky I am. Because I feel lucky, I act in a confident, positive way, and as a result, good things tend to occur. I hope you'll experiment with some of the items you read about in this book, and see how lucky you become while using them.

How to Use This Book

This book is divided into four parts. Part one discusses a variety of ways to attract luck into your life by changing your attitude and approach to life. Most of these are simple adjustments that will help you find new and fresh opportunities that may well prove lucky for you. Part two explores some of the traditional methods used to attract good luck, such as magical words, gemstones, and lucky charms. No matter what your view may be on these, you'll find it an interesting exercise to choose one or two to experiment with. Part three looks at how to create luck in the important areas of love, marriage, and the home. As luck often involves timing, this part also looks at the seasons, days, months, and years. Part four discusses the folk traditions concerning luck. These include lucky animals, food and drink, and folklore. It also looks at luck in Asia, as people there have been examining different ways to attract and enhance good luck for thousands of years.

You can use this book in a number of ways. You might read it from start to finish. Alternatively, you might start by reading the entries that interest you the most before looking at some of the others. You might prefer to dip into the book at random and see what you find. You might keep it as a reference book and flip through it occasionally. There are enough entries to try something different every day for a whole year, if that is what you'd like to do. No matter how you use it, I hope you'll find a number of ways to help you create good luck well before you finish the book.

— Part One —

Taking Action for Luck

When I first entered the workforce, it didn't take me long to discover that the most successful people in the corporation were different from the others. They were self-motivated, goal-oriented, positive, enthusiastic, and hardworking. They made an effort to get along with everyone and were open, friendly, and encouraging. The rest of the staff seemed half alive in comparison. They did enough work to keep their jobs, but little more. They demonstrated enthusiasm and initiative sometimes, but appeared unable to sustain these qualities for any length of time.

At a company function, I gathered up enough courage to ask one of the sales managers, Mr. Wilshin, how he managed to remain positive and motivated all the time. He was happy to tell me. "Every morning, I look into my bathroom mirror and say to myself, 'Boy, I'm enthusiastic!'" He pumped his hands vigorously in the air to demonstrate exactly what he did. "I do that three times, each time louder and more enthusiastically than the time before. That keeps me motivated and enthusiastic all day long. It makes me lucky, too."

I've thought about Mr. Wilshin a great deal over the years, and followed his career with great interest. He worked in increasingly senior positions in several countries, and finished his career as president of a large multinational company. I experimented myself and found his method of motivation works well. I'd love to know how many of the other ideas in this section he also used, consciously or unconsciously. Mr. Wilshin definitely took action for luck, and it paid off. This section contains fifty-nine ways in which you can take action to create good luck. They've worked for me, and I know they will work for you, too.

One

....

Your Amazing Biology

Introduction

The Scottish philosopher Sydney Banks (1931–2009) taught that we're only ever one thought away from feeling happy or sad.[1] We all have the ability to control our thoughts, but few people consciously direct their thoughts toward happiness. How we think has a direct bearing on how lucky we are. It's possible to paraphrase Syd Banks and say that we're only one thought away from feeling lucky or unlucky. Someone who thinks he or she is lucky will experience more luck in life than someone who constantly feels he or she is unlucky. This is because we attract to us whatever it is we concentrate on. Scientists have discovered that our brains continue to develop throughout life. By changing the way we think, we can achieve almost anything we desire.

Not long ago, I watched a soccer game with my eleven-year-old grandson. He adores the game, and I'm sure he'd love to become a professional footballer when he grows up. Until recently, I believed that exceptional sports people were born with special talents and most of us could never hope to emulate their particular skills. However, if I'd played soccer at school, loved the game, participated in every opportunity to improve my skills that I could, practiced constantly, and remained totally focused on the goal of becoming a professional player, who knows what might have happened. Many of us blame our lack of success on bad genes, a belief that ensures we remain watching from the bleachers, rather than playing on the field.

Other factors come into play, too. Desire and motivation are essential for anyone wanting success in any field. A young man I know was an extremely talented swimmer. For years, he got up early every morning to train. After school, when his friends were having fun, he'd be back in the pool training again. I was surprised when he suddenly gave it up.

"I realized the price was too high," he told me. "I thought I wanted to be a champion swimmer, but I didn't want it that much." It turned out he was following his father's dream. I'm sure he'd have carried on if he'd been pursuing his own dream, as that would have provided him with the necessary motivation. Of course, if he had carried on and succeeded, everyone would have said how lucky he was. They wouldn't think of the countless hours he'd spent training and preparing for success; he'd simply be "lucky."

If you're prepared to pay the price, you can be "lucky" at your chosen sport. Over time, as you practice and train, your physical body will change, and the muscles required for your particular sport will develop.

In addition to the human body, your brain will also change to reflect what you're working on. You are not limited by your IQ (intelligence quotient). Your intellectual ability can be measured at any time, but it's impossible to measure your potential, which is unlimited. The science of neuroplasticity proves that your brain constantly changes and grows all the way through life. Consequently, the report cards you received during your school days have no bearing on the person you are today. If you say you can't do something because you're "not smart enough," you'll be correct—you're holding yourself back from your true potential. While you may blame your lack of success on your bad genes or lack of education, the reality is that you're smart enough to achieve anything you set your mind on, assuming you want it badly enough. If you set a worthwhile goal, motivate yourself, and do the necessary work, you'll achieve success. Interestingly, people will ignore or forget about the hard work you put in to achieve your goal, and will simply describe you as "lucky." I remember seeing Engelbert Humperdinck on television shortly after he became successful in the 1960s. He didn't like being referred to as an "overnight success," as he'd put in many years of hard work before he became famous.

The American psychologist Lewis Terman (1877–1956) was a professor of Educational Psychology at Stanford University when he adapted and standardized the IQ test. In the 1920s, he started a thirty-five-year study of children with high IQs. He believed that children blessed with exceptional genes would lead highly successful lives. His 1,500 test subjects did become healthy, successful adults. However, none of them won a Nobel Prize or became a world-famous musician. Interestingly enough, two people who were rejected from Terman's original group did win the Nobel Prize, and Isaac Stern and Yehudi Menuhin— both rejected—grew up to become internationally famous violinists.[2]

In 1993, Norihiro Sadato, a Japanese scientist, discovered that when blind people read Braille, the visual cortex of their brains lit up on PET scans. This demonstrated that this area of the brain had changed as a result of the loss of sight. In fact, it was essential that this area of the brain changed to allow these people to read Braille. This is one example of the brain's plasticity.[3]

In 1999, Dr. Eleanor Maguire, a British neurologist, performed MRI scans on London taxi drivers, and found they had much larger posterior hippocampi than the people she also scanned who were not driving taxis. The posterior (or rear) hippocampus section of the brain relates to navigation.

To become a licensed taxi driver in London, you need to memorize all 25,000 streets in central London, and also know all the points of interest on each one. This information is known as "the Knowledge," and it takes the average person two to four years (and twelve attempts), before he or she is fully licensed. It's a remarkable feat of memory. Eleanor Maguire discovered that the size of each taxi drivers' posterior hippocampus was related to the length of the person's driving career. This finding indicates that the brain grows as information is acquired.[4]

Even imagining you're doing something affects the motor cortex of the brain. Dr. Alvaro Pascual-Leone, currently professor of Neurology at Harvard Medical School, asked a group of volunteers to imagine they were practicing a simple piece of music on a piano. They did this every day for five days. Interestingly, the part of the motor cortex that controls the movement of the fingers expanded in the brains of the volunteers in exactly the same way as it did in the brains of people who actually played the piece.[5] This experiment demonstrates that thoughts have the power to change the physical structure of the brain.

So it follows that what you think about luck is reflected in the makeup of your brain. If you're not happy with any aspect of your life, you can change the way you think about it, and this will effectively rewire your brain. Consequently, if you feel you're unlucky, you can turn this around completely and start thinking like a "lucky" person. Positive thinking works. It takes time, but focusing on the positive rather than the negative ultimately affects the brain's makeup.

There's an interesting exercise you can do which demonstrates the power of positive thinking. In the evening, before going to bed, sit down quietly in a comfortable chair, close your eyes, and relax. Take ten slow, deep breaths, and then think about the day you've just had. Think about the people you've interacted with, and your responses to them. Think about the frustrations you experienced, as well as the accomplishments. Once you've covered all the main events of the day, take three slow, deep breaths, and open your eyes. Spend a few minutes thinking about what you've just done. Did you feel anything in your body while you were reliving the day? Did you feel tense or angry with anything you thought about?

Stand up, stretch, and maybe walk around the house for a minute or two. Sit down again, close your eyes, relax, take ten slow, deep breaths, and go through your day again. However, this time, you're going to put a positive slant on everything that occurred. If, for instance, someone cut you off in traffic on your way to work, you probably tensed up as you recalled your commute. This time, simply wish the person well. Remind yourself that the driver had no power to affect your thoughts. You allowed yourself to become angry. As you relive the experience, let your negativity float away, and see yourself calm and relaxed, instead of angry and frustrated. Continue going through your day, putting a positive slant on everything that happened. When you've finished, take three slow, deep breaths, and open your eyes.

Again spend a few minutes thinking about what you've just done. Did you notice any stress or frustration in your body as you relived your day from a positive point of view?

You can release any negativity by reliving the experience and seeing it work out exactly the way you wanted it to. By releasing negativity and adopting a more positive outlook on life, you'll notice changes in every area of your life.

We're lucky that we have the ability to effectively reprogram our brains, and become the person we want to be. It's never too late, either. Some people develop their talents early in life. Wolfgang Amadeus Mozart (1756–1791), for instance, is a good example of a child prodigy. We hear more about child prodigies than we do about "late bloomers."

Anna Mary Robertson Moses, better known as Grandma Moses (1860–1961), the famous American folk artist, took up painting in her seventies and was still painting in her nineties. André Kertész (1894–1985), the Hungarian-born American photographer, didn't become famous until he was in his eighties. Colonel Harlan Sanders (1890–1980) started franchising Kentucky Fried Chicken when he was sixty-five. Child prodigies are rare, but there are many late bloomers.

In the next chapter, we'll look at different methods you can use to take control of your luck.

Two

....

How to Take Control of Your Luck

Introduction

This chapter contains fifty-nine practical ways to increase your luck. They can be read in any order you wish. You might like to read the chapter and then decide which ones you'd like to experiment with first. Alternatively, something might interest you, and you might decide to start with that one first. You'll make faster progress if you work on one or two at a time, rather than trying to do too many. Focus on these until you notice some improvement, and then add another, and another, until you've worked on all the areas you need help with.

Some of these ideas need a change in outlook, but others involve looking for opportunities to put them into practice. Number 27: The Harder You Work, the Luckier You Get is an example. To gain the most from this idea, you should volunteer for any task that involves persistence and hard work. If this isn't possible, tackle a task you've been putting off. Work hard until you've completed it, and enjoy the satisfaction of finishing something that was difficult or not particularly pleasant. Recently, I cleared all the junk out of our garage. This was a chore I'd put off for years. I found something I thought I'd lost, which was lucky for me, and two months later, my wife and I still gain pleasure every time we drive in or out of our garage.

1. Attitude

Joseph Addison (1672–1719), the English essayist, wrote: "I never knew an early-rising, hard-working, prudent man, careful of his earnings, and strictly honest, who complained of bad luck. A good character, good habits, and iron industry are impregnable to the assaults of all the ill-luck that fools ever dreamed of." Joseph Addison obviously had a positive attitude.

Everyone has an attitude. Some people are born with a positive attitude and have an optimistic approach to life. Other people are born with a gloomier disposition, which gives them a negative attitude.

At one time I worked in a warehouse at a printing supplies company. The woman who prepared the invoices was one of the most negative people I've ever met. Nothing was good in her life, and she loved telling everyone about her problems. At work, she enjoyed creating problems whenever she could. She also enjoyed dragging everyone down to her level. If you commented on the beautiful day, she'd reply: "The weather forecast says it will rain tomorrow." I worked there for three months, and for most of that time tried to make her smile. I didn't succeed, and I assume she's still wallowing in her negativity.

Shortly after leaving the warehouse, we moved house. I had a small mail order business and visited the local post office several times a week. Most of the staff were pleasant and friendly to deal with. However, one lady was grumpy and appeared to go out of her way to make life difficult for the customers. Remembering the lady in the warehouse, I made it my goal to make her smile. It took almost three years to achieve this. Twenty years later, she's still at the post office. Whenever I walk in, she smiles and waves to me, but she's unpleasant to everyone else. It taught me that I have the power to change my own attitude, but it's impossible to change anyone else's. They have to decide to do it themselves.

There's a famous story about two people who look at a half-filled glass of water. One person sees the container as half empty; the other sees it half full. The first person has a pessimistic approach to life, while the second is an optimist. Which of these two people is more likely to be lucky? The optimist expects good things to happen, and as a result, is much more likely to experience apparent luck than a pessimistic colleague. The optimist has a good attitude, and attitude is everything.

With a good attitude, optimists feels good about themselves, and are able to look ahead and make plans for the future. Pessimists are so full of anxieties and doubts that their minds are too occupied to think about future plans.

Most people's attitudes vary from time to time. No one is 100 percent positive all the time. The key to success is to be positive more often than negative. In fact, we always have a choice. Any time you're feeling negative, you can deliberately change your attitude and make it more positive. You'll feel much better as a result. There'll be less stress, and you'll lead a much more enjoyable, more relaxed life.

Attitude is important in every area of life. Let's imagine two men at a party. One is an optimist and the other is a pessimist. They both see an attractive lady. The optimist thinks: "The worst thing that can happen is she'll turn me down." He walks over and introduces himself. The pessimist thinks: "She's bound to turn me down. Why humiliate myself?" As a result, he doesn't introduce himself and misses out on an opportunity to make a new friend.

Let's imagine the same two people at work. They're both faced with a problem. The optimist thinks: "Let's look at this from another angle. There has to be a solution." The pessimist thinks: "Let's give up now. It's impossible." The pessimist gives up; the optimist persists until she succeeds.

When I told a friend I was working on this chapter, he told me: "Attitude isn't just important; it's essential. It plays a major part in everything you do. No one achieves success in any area of life without a good attitude. Your attitude determines how successful you'll become. If you have a good attitude, you can't help but be lucky." My friend is a joy to be around, as he's always cheerful and positive. He's had as many ups and downs as anyone, but consciously decides to make every day a good one.

Optimists enjoy being with other optimists. They expect good things to happen. They spend as little time as possible with negative people, as they know moaners and complainers enjoy pulling everyone down to their level. One morning a week I go to a breakfast club meeting. I joined it fifteen years ago as I felt the need to mix with positive, enthusiastic people. I had become sick and tired of the constant negativity of a magic club I belonged to, and joined the breakfast club the same week I resigned from the magic club. It's been interesting to watch the growth and development of the members of the breakfast club over the last ten years, compared with the members of the magic club. The bickering, infighting, and petty jealousies have prevented the magic club members from progressing in their careers, while the breakfast club members are achieving their goals and succeeding in every area of their lives.

I've thought about these two groups many times over the past decade. I occasionally come across people who still belong to the magic club, and they're always keen to tell me the latest gossip about the other members. Members of the breakfast club are too busy pursuing their goals to waste time in negativity and gossip.

More than twenty years ago, Dr. Martin E. P. Seligman conducted a series of experiments with salespeople at Metropolitan Life. Not surprisingly, the optimists turned out to be more successful than the pessimists. Dr. Seligman believed that it was the person's self-talk that either sustained or defeated the salespeople as they made their daily cold calls on the phone. Someone who thought "No one wants to buy insurance from me" would give up quickly after a few knockbacks. However, the salesperson who thought "They may already have insurance, but eight out of ten people are uninsured" would keep on making calls.

Encouraged by this discovery, Metropolitan Life carried out a larger test on all fifteen thousand people who applied for sales positions in 1985. They employed one thousand of these without using Dr. Seligman's optimism test. Dr. Seligman wanted to use this data later on to see if the optimists outperformed the pessimists. In fact, they did. In the first year, the optimists outsold the pessimists by 8 percent, and this increased to 30 percent in the second year.

Dr. Seligman also performed another experiment, asking the insurance company to employ one hundred people who had failed the entrance criteria, but were rated super-optimists on Dr. Seligman's test. These people would not normally have been offered a position in the company. Their results were amazing. In the first year, they outsold the pessimists by 21 percent and this rose to 57 perecnt in the second year. This conclusively demonstrated that optimists make much better salespeople than pessimists.[1]

If you maintain a positive attitude, you'll not only enjoy a happier life, but you'll also be significantly luckier than people with a negative attitude. This is because you'll be open to any opportunities that come your way. You'll be more approachable and develop a wider circle of friends, which will also provide you with more opportunities.

2. Take Control

You need to take control of your thoughts, as these influence your attitude and actions. Ultimately, your thoughts will attract or repel good luck. Most people pay little attention to how positive or negative their thoughts are. You'll be amazed at the difference in your attitude toward every aspect of your life once you start focusing on positive thoughts. Naturally, you'll find yourself thinking negative thoughts every now and again. You don't need to berate yourself when this occurs. Simply switch your thoughts around and think of something positive. Each time you do this, the more positive you'll become. In time, the process will become automatic. One technique I found useful when working as a salesman was to think about a major sale I'd made immediately before approaching another prospect. The memory of the past success gave me the right attitude to make another sale. Naturally, when I made the additional sale, my colleagues attributed it to good luck.

You should also constantly see yourself as being in control of your destiny. This means you'll take ownership of every situation, good and bad, and will remain focused on progressing toward your goals. People who do the opposite and think of themselves as powerless victims lead lives of frustration and blame everyone else for their misfortunes and lack of success. Once you realize that you're in control of your destiny, everything will start to go your way, and you'll be luckier than ever before.

3. Associate with Like-Minded People

Other people affect your thoughts and actions. Negative people try to pull you down and encourage you to share their negativity. I call them vampires, as they have the ability to suck out every trace of positivity. Nurture your relationships with positive people, and spend as little time as possible with negative vampires.

4. Find a Magnificent Obsession

We all need something worthwhile to aim for. Find something challenging, stimulating, and worthy of your time and effort. This will be different for everyone. One person might find this in studying toward a degree, while another might achieve the same satisfaction in seeking a closer connection with the divine, or in helping people less fortunate than him- or herself. One person I know began a program of self-development and started working on resolving his inappropriate responses whenever he felt angry or impatient.

5. Set Goals and Achieve Them

This is a continuation of seeking a magnificent obsession. The most successful people, usually called the luckiest people, choose worthwhile goals, and then work hard until they've achieved them. Usually, they have a number of goals. Some are short-term while others might take a lifetime to achieve. Some are relatively easy to achieve, while others are difficult. Achieving short-term and easier goals keeps these people motivated as they strive to achieve their more difficult, long-term goals. If you set challenging, worthwhile goals for yourself and work hard to attain them, you'll be amazed at how lucky you become.

6. Be Happy

The great American president Abraham Lincoln (1809–1865) said, "Most people are about as happy as they make up their mind to be." I'm sure that, like me, you know many people who go through life appearing to be unhappy, while others, often with much less to be happy about, seem to be in constant good spirits.

Many years ago, Tai Lau, a feng shui master, told me, "If you want to be happy, be happy." It was simple yet very profound advice, and I've tried to follow it ever since. Every morning when I wake up, I tell myself that I'm going to enjoy a wonderful day. I've found that starting the day with positive thoughts makes me feel good and enables me to remain happy no matter what the day brings. It's not easy to remain happy in the midst of the various challenges we all face as we go through life. It's a sign of maturity to take control of your own happiness and be happy, no matter what.

I've found that maintaining a positive, happy disposition makes me luckier in many different ways. I seldom have problems finding a parking space close to where I want to be when I go downtown, for instance. I feel confident that I'll find a parking space, and I usually do. Recently, I went to a wine tasting at my local wine shop and was fortunate enough to buy the last bottle of the wine he had opened for tasting. The owner told me I was lucky, and reminded me that I'd done exactly the same thing a year or two earlier. I already felt happy at obtaining the last bottle, but it was good to have the luck aspect reinforced as well.

7. Use Positive Affirmations

Affirmations are words that are repeated over and over to instill positive thoughts into our minds. They are always phrased in the present tense and stated strongly, as if whatever it is you're saying is already true.

You might, for instance, be suffering from a lack of confidence. To correct this difficulty, you might say to yourself as many times a day as possible: "I am confident and strong. I can stand up for myself in any type of situation." Obviously, this won't be the case when you start saying this affirmation. However, if you keep repeating it, it will ultimately become part of your reality, and you'll gain the confidence you need.

You can do exactly the same thing with luck. If you constantly repeat: "I am lucky. Good things happen to me all the time," you will improve your luck.

The trick is to keep control over your thoughts. Anything you say can become an affirmation. If you constantly say to yourself, "I'm never lucky," or "life isn't fair," that will become your reality.

Consequently, it's vitally important to think positively as much as possible. During the course of an average day, we all think a mixture of positive, neutral, and negative thoughts. If you find yourself thinking a negative thought, deliberately turn it around and make it positive, or alternatively, think about something different instead.

Here are some positive affirmations that will help improve your luck:

+ "I'm worthy of the very best life has to offer."

+ "I attract good things to me."

+ "I allow myself to make the most of every moment."

+ "I'm alive, I'm well, and I feel great."

8. Spend Time with Friends

A short while ago, a relative of mine told me that he had no friends. He had devoted his life to making money and although he'd been extremely successful at this, he wasn't happy. I felt sad for him, as good friends are amongst the greatest blessings life has to offer.

As I work at home, it would be easy to focus on my work and gradually become a hermit. Fortunately, I keep in regular contact with my friends. I usually meet them for morning coffee or lunch. When I return home and get back to work, I'm happy, stimulated, and more productive. Although it's not the reason why I meet them, my friends often give me good ideas and suggestions.

Recently, I happened to mention I was writing a book on a particular subject. My friend said he knew someone who had been involved in this field for many years and would I like to meet him? This chance remark led to a meeting with a charming man who gave me some excellent ideas for the book. Meeting him was a lucky day for me. I've had many experiences like this over the years.

9. Make New Friends

As well as nurturing your current friendships, you should nurture all your relationships, and be willing to accept new people into your life. Naturally, you should nurture these, too. You should do this with no expectation of any reward, other than the new friendships you might make. However, each of these new friends has other friends, and your circle of contacts will steadily grow. The more contacts you have, the more opportunities you'll have. Over a period of time, you'll be amazed at how lucky you become. It's been estimated that the average American has approximately 300 contacts. Some of these are strong, such as family and good friends. Others are more tenuous, and include people you deal with at the bank and post office, gas station attendants, and the like. As each of these people is also in contact with 300 others, you're a maximum of one step away from 90,000 people. You can take that even further, too. If all of those people have 300 contacts, you're a maximum of two steps away from 27,000,000 people!

It's not hard to make friends. Be sociable, accept invitations, and make the first move when you meet people you like.

10. Expect Serendipity

Serendipity is the act of finding something useful or valuable without searching for it. I've experienced this frequently in bookstores and libraries. While looking for a particular book, I often find another book that is even more helpful than the book I was searching for.

The word *serendipity* was coined by the English writer Horace Walpole (1717–1797), after reading *The Three Princes of Serendip*, a Persian fairy tale in which the three heroes constantly made interesting discoveries by accident.

Something I find fascinating about serendipity is that my luck improves if I expect serendipity to occur. Whenever I visit a library, for instance, I wonder what books I'll discover by accident. Because I expect to make interesting discoveries, I find them regularly.

While writing this section, I read in today's newspaper a human interest piece about a man having his hair cut. He happened to mention that his house was damp, and the hairdresser said that he'd installed a certain type of heat pump. A man having his hair cut in the next chair commented that he sold and installed this particular heat pump, and the man with the damp house immediately employed him. This was serendipitous for both the man with the damp house and the man who sold heat pumps. It was also serendipitous for me to read this at the exact time I was writing about serendipity.[2]

The Greek mathematician Archimedes had a serendipitous moment in the public baths of Syracuse. Apparently, he ran naked through the streets of Syracuse calling out, "Eureka!" ("I've found it!") Archimedes accidentally discovered that the amount of water that spilled out of his bath was exactly equal to the bulk of the part of his body that was submerged.[3]

A few years ago, I was fortunate enough to visit the Lascaux Caves near Montignac in southwestern France. These caves were discovered accidentally by four boys who were exploring the woods near their home. They widened a small hole they found in the ground, and crawled into a large space. They were amazed to see beautiful paintings of animals on the walls.

The Dead Sea Scrolls were discovered in 1947 by a young boy who was looking for a lost goat. These are excellent examples of something wonderful being discovered by accident.

Expect fortunate things to happen by accident. They will, and everyone will tell you how lucky you are.

11. Nurture Yourself

Most people lead busy lives, and it can be difficult to take time out purely to nurture themselves. However, it's vitally important for your happiness and well-being to nurture your physical, emotional, and spiritual selves. Nurturing yourself has nothing to do with self-indulgence. Nurturing is loving, respecting, caring, and respecting yourself for the magnificent creation that you are.

Nurturing yourself means that you have a right to do something special for yourself every day. This could be as simple as going for a walk and leaving your cell phone at home. It might be buying flowers for no reason at all. It could be phoning a friend for a chat. It might be setting aside ten minutes to read a book. It could be listing in your mind all the blessings in your life. It might even be simply spending time on your own. Changing your daily routine is a good way to nurture yourself. One of the best ways to nurture yourself is to slow down. When you slow down even for a minute or two, you'll be able to see all the things you normally miss as you race through your day.

You can nurture yourself by helping others. This can be as small as smiling at a stranger as you pass in the street. It can be a kind word. It can be a donation of time or money. Often, spending time with someone can be a priceless gift. You nurture yourself when you accept other people as they are. You also nurture yourself when you don't always have to be right. Go with the flow.

How does nurturing yourself improve your luck? When you feel good about yourself (and nurturing yourself certainly does that), you're receptive to all the good things life has to offer, and good things will start coming your way.

12. Laugh More

I regularly watch stand-up comedians on YouTube. I love to laugh, as it invigorates me, releases tension, and makes me feel good. It reminds me how good it is to be alive.

Children laugh much more than adults. Although estimates vary, it's said that children laugh 300 to 400 times a day. Apparently, adults laugh fifteen to twenty times. Obviously, everyone is different, but there's no doubt that children laugh much more than adults.

In his book, *Anatomy of an Illness*, Norman Cousins described how watching old Marx Brothers movies helped him reduce both pain and inflammation. In fact, ten minutes of laughter brought him two hours of restful, pain-free sleep. It's no wonder laughter has been called the best medicine.

Laughter relaxes the entire body, reduces stress levels, and improves blood flow to the heart. It also produces endorphins (which make us feel good) and antibodies that help fight infection. A good laugh is extremely beneficial from a health point of view.

Laughing also keeps you young. Michael Pritchard is famous for saying: "You don't stop laughing because you grow old. You grow old because you stop laughing."

When you laugh, you become more optimistic, outgoing, and friendlier. You also become more attractive to others. Laughing is contagious, and every time you laugh you have the potential to help others as well as yourself. Laughing with others also increases your connection with them, and opens doors for new experiences and opportunities. This increases your potential for good luck.

Seize every opportunity you can to laugh, and make it a good one if you can.

13. Expect Good Things to Happen

This relates to maintaining a positive mental attitude. If you believe good things will happen, you won't be devastated by the mistakes and failures that everyone experiences from time to time. Instead you'll be convinced that something good will come out of the situation and, as you expect that to happen, you'll be alert to every opportunity that presents itself.

Good things can be both small and large. A few months ago, I happened to walk past a house while a children's birthday party was in progress. About a dozen girls were playing a game on the front lawn, watched by several parents. One of the girls was holding a daisy. As I walked past, she ran over and presented it to me.

14. Act As If You Are Lucky

Everyone's heard the phrase "fake it until you make it." Our minds are extremely suggestible. If you constantly act as if you're lucky, and affirm this to yourself all the time, you'll find that you will become lucky. When you act as if you're lucky, you attract good luck to you, and luck will become a reality in your life.

A friend of mine regularly finds money on the street. On several occasions while I've been walking with her, she's suddenly bent down and picked up a coin or note that someone had dropped. Each time, I would have walked past without seeing it. When I asked her about her useful talent, she told me she'd always been lucky at finding money.

15. Eliminate Negative Emotions

It's hard to be lucky when you're crippled by shyness or feelings of jealousy or rage. They prevent you from moving ahead, as your mind constantly dwells on your own perceived limitations. These feelings can also be seen by others. As negativity of any sort is unattractive, emotions of this sort can prevent people from helping you.

It's natural to feel negative when events seem to be conspiring against you, but it's one thing to feel them, and quite another to express them. When you eliminate the negativity, you increase your opportunities of attracting all the good things of life, including good luck.

16. The World Is Your Oyster

You're not going to experience much luck if you stay at home, and fail to venture out into the world. There are opportunities everywhere, but you need to be out and about to find them.

Of course, you'll make mistakes when you move out of your comfort zone. Everyone makes mistakes. One man I know told me that he loves making mistakes, as each one brings him ever closer to success. When I queried him about this, he told me that he learned from every mistake, and this told him what not to do next time.

Just recently, a friend of mine phoned someone who owned a valuable art collection. It had taken him several months to gather the necessary courage to make the call. My friend is keen on art and wanted to see in particular a certain painting the man owned. When my friend finally phoned, he was immediately invited to the art collector's house to see the entire collection.

Be brave. Take chances. Trust. The world truly is your oyster.

17. Eliminate Envy

We've all experienced situations in which someone else got the promotion, even though we thought we were better suited for the position. There's no point in being envious of the person who got the job. After all, the new position might be incredibly stressful, or involve more hours of work each week than you'd be prepared to put in.

It's a similar situation if a friend has a gorgeous partner while you're still on your own. The partner might look attractive but could be extremely needy and hard to live with. What you think is your friend's good luck might in reality be the opposite.

Instead of feeling jealous or envious of someone else's apparent good luck, remain focused on your own hopes and dreams.

18. Remember the Good Things

Many years ago, a man came to me for help with insomnia. I discovered that when he went to bed at night, he'd think about the mistakes he'd made during the day. After that, he'd think about the silly things he'd done over the previous few days, and then move back to the previous month. He'd keep going back in time until he was thinking about the stupid things he'd done as a small child. No wonder he couldn't fall asleep! I taught him to think about all the good things that had happened to him during the day, and his problem ceased. Meeting this man made me wonder how many people limit their lives by constantly reliving all the unpleasant, shameful, negative, and unhappy experiences from their past.

To be lucky, you must develop a selective memory. Remember the good things. Relive them with a smile on your face. Count your blessings and realize how lucky you actually are.

19. Forgive

It's impossible to move ahead if you're constantly dwelling on something negative from the past. Everyone has experienced hurt, and it's natural to feel anger, resentment, and fear that it could happen again. However, there's no law that says you must hang on to those feelings forever. If you do, you're effectively stuck in the past. You can't move on until you let go and forgive the other person. When you forgive, you set yourself free. This means you can move ahead again.

Failing to forgive keeps you imprisoned in your own personal hell, constantly going over past grievances and hurts. Lucky people have no time for that. They're constantly looking ahead rather than living in the past.

While you're forgiving others, forgive yourself as well. No one is perfect, and everyone is doing the best he or she can.

20. Be Grateful

When you make an effort to look for the good in every situation and be grateful for it, you'll become aware of how lucky you actually are right now.

Here's a small example. While writing this section my phone rang. When I answered it, the person asked for someone I didn't know. When I told him he'd dialed the wrong number, the man on the other end didn't apologize. In fact, he didn't say anything. He hung up on me while I was still talking. At one time I would have thought about this incident for some time, thinking about how rude he'd been. Now, instead of doing that, I silently thanked him. His call had forced me out of my chair and given me a brief break from my computer screen.

Express your gratitude to your family and friends. Recognize their importance in your life. Be grateful for your job. Even if the pay is low, be grateful. Be grateful for the gift of life. Be grateful for being you.

Dr. Martin Seligman, former president of the American Psychological Association, created a gratitude exercise known as the "Three Blessings." At the end of each day, he suggests that you think about the three things that occurred during the day that you're most happy about. This simple technique helps to reduce feelings of anxiety and depression and at the same time increase feelings of joy and happiness.[4]

Dr. Robert Emmons, a professor at the University of California and author of a number of books on gratitude, conducted a lengthy project called the Gratitude Interventions Project.[5] He discovered that people who expressed gratitude were happier, healthier, more enthusiastic, and more energetic than people who didn't. They were also more successful at setting and achieving goals.[6]

Actively look for opportunities to thank people. It makes you feel good, and is appreciated by others. It also makes you memorable and may provide you with further opportunities in the future.

21. Take Chances

You won't succeed if you never try anything. Take a chance. Even if it doesn't pay off, you'll learn from the experience. Taking a chance means taking risks. This doesn't necessarily mean crossing Niagara Falls on a tightrope—it could be making the first move and introducing yourself to a stranger at a function you're attending. It might be being brave enough to ask for a pay rise.

Naturally, you should try to minimize the risk and avoid anything foolhardy or dangerous. Evaluate the situation carefully, take a calculated risk, and move forward.

22. Keep Your Sense of Wonder

It's easy to forget how incredibly fortunate we all are to be alive today, living on this amazing planet full of incredible variety and diversity. Try going outside on a cloudless evening, and gaze up at the stars. Visit a nearby scenic lookout and marvel at the magnificent view. Watch a flock of birds flying in unison. Walk along a beach. Appreciate the laughter of children. Play with a pet. We're surrounded by wonder. Pause and appreciate it every now and again. Pausing to appreciate the wonders all around you will help you realize just how lucky you are.

23. Spend Time on Your Own

Take time out of your daily schedule to relax on your own. Although it might be hard, it's especially important to do this when you're really busy. You'll be amazed at the ideas that will come to you when you sit quietly and think about your hopes and dreams. Don't sit down and let your mind wander. If possible, think about ideas that will help you solve a problem. It doesn't have to be a particular problem of yours. Think of ideas you could implement that would make other people's lives easier or more comfortable. Don't evaluate the ideas as you get them. Write them all down, and think about them later.

You may choose to spend time on your own working at a hobby, exercising, or doing something else you enjoy. You'll find good ideas will come to you no matter what you're doing.

24. Meditate

Setting aside time on your own to think is highly beneficial. You can increase the benefits of this by learning how to meditate. The word *meditate* comes from the Latin word *medi*, which means "to center." Consequently, when you meditate you go within and align yourself with the center of your being.

Meditation has many benefits. It quietens the mind, improves mental health, strengthens the immune system, and reduces stress, depression, backaches, and negativity.

There are many ways to meditate. Some people do it through walking, jogging, gardening, or gazing at a beautiful scene. Other people meditate by losing themselves in a hobby. In all of these examples, the participants are in a state of mindfulness. They are living in the moment, free from all worries and concerns.

One of the simplest ways to meditate is to sit in a comfortable chair, and take several slow, deep breaths through your nose. I like to close my eyes while doing this, but many people prefer to gaze at a burning candle, or a tranquil scene. Allow yourself to relax with each exhalation, and feel all the muscles in your body gradually becoming loose and limp.

You'll probably notice random thoughts coming into your mind from time to time. When you become aware of them, gently dismiss them by focusing on your breathing.

When you feel completely relaxed, allow your mind to think of the word *luck*. Various thoughts and ideas will come into your mind. If you find your mind thinking about matters that are totally unrelated to luck, focus on your breathing for a few seconds and silently say the word *luck* to yourself.

When you feel ready, finish the meditation with a brief prayer of thanks to the Architect of the Universe. Open your eyes and continue relaxing for a minute or two, until you feel ready to get up again.

It takes practice to relax and slow down your thoughts. Remain patient when your mind drifts away. Gently bring your attention back to the meditation. If you give yourself ten or fifteen minutes a day to meditate, you'll be amazed at how much better you'll feel about every aspect of your life. You'll find yourself feeling more relaxed, less anxious, and more accepting and understanding. You'll also feel—and become—luckier.

25. Persist

Frequently, the most successful people are those who refuse to quit. They persevere long after most people would have given up. Calvin Coolidge (1872–1933), the American president, was convinced of the power of persistence. He wrote: "Nothing in the world can take the place of Persistence. Talent will not; nothing is more common than unsuccessful men with talent. Genius will not; unrewarded genius is almost a proverb. Education will not; the world is full of educated derelicts. Persistence and determination alone are omnipotent. The slogan 'Press on' has solved and always will solve the problems of the human race."

It's natural for your motivation to waver when you're working on a large-scale goal or project. It's impossible to remain motivated all the time. Consequently, many people give up as it seems too hard, and the goal appears too far away. Persistent people keep on working, even when the goal seems impossible to achieve.

A strange thing happens when these people achieve success: everyone forgets the months or years of hard work and effort and says how lucky they are.

26. Find the Silver Lining

Whenever you find yourself in a difficult situation, look for the silver lining in the cloud that's covering you. It might take time to find it, but it will be there. It might come in the form of a lesson, a new insight, or even a hidden benefit.

One advantage of looking for the silver lining is that your attitude will immediately change. Instead of thinking gloomy thoughts, you'll be reaffirming your belief in yourself and start moving forward again. This means you'll be taking control again, rather than allowing circumstances to rule your life.

27. The Harder You Work, the Luckier You Get

Gary Player, the South African golfer, is one of several people who have been credited with coining the phrase "The harder you work, the luckier you get."[7] This means that when you work hard, you'll discover lucky opportunities that will be missed by people who do as little work as possible. Interestingly, as opportunities that involve hard work are ignored by most people, there is less competition to worry about.

28. Do Something New

A few months ago, I visited a friend and noticed he was reading a book on cabinet-making. As I've never seen him do anything remotely practical, I asked him why he chose that particular book. He told me that once a month he takes a book out of his local library on a subject he knows nothing about. He finds some interesting, and others he discards after reading a few chapters.

"It keeps me mentally stimulated, and also gives me great ideas," he said with a smile.

Another friend of mine has started learning the piano at the age of seventy-five. "It keeps me young," she told me.

Learning and doing new things will keep you mentally stimulated and youthful in outlook. It also exposes you to new ideas and concepts that have the potential to increase your luck.

29. Look for Opportunities

Russell Conwell (1843–1925), an American Baptist minister, philanthropist, and author, wrote a powerful speech called "Acres of Diamonds." He presented it more than six thousand times, and it was published as a book in 1890.[8] In the speech, Conwell tells of a man who sold his property so he could look for diamonds. The person who bought it later discovered a fortune in diamonds beneath his property. In fact, it was the largest diamond find in history, and became the Kimberly Diamond Mine. The message is that you don't have to travel to find opportunities; they are everywhere.

Every time you experience a problem, think about the potential opportunities it provides. Your solution could prove rewarding in many different ways.

A good way to find opportunities is to ask questions. Why is something done in a certain way? Why can't I buy such-and-such locally? When you find a good opportunity and take advantage of it, your friends will tell you how lucky you are.

Once you start actively looking for opportunities, you'll find they pop up everywhere, even when you're not looking for them.

30. Charisma

People who have personalities that naturally appeal to others are said to be charismatic. "Charisma" comes from the Greek word *khárisma*, which means "gift of grace." Max Weber (1864–1920), the German sociologist, wrote: "Charisma is a certain quality of an individual personality by virtue of which he is set apart from ordinary men and treated as endowed with supernatural, superhuman, or at least specifically exceptional powers or qualities."[9] This makes it sound as if charisma is possessed by a few lucky people, but fortunately, everyone can become more charismatic if they want to be. The secret of charisma is basically liking others. If you genuinely like people, you'll be interested in them and it will be expressed in your words, actions, and facial expressions. Smile, look people in the eye, relax, listen, and be yourself.

When you look at someone or something you like, the pupils in your eyes dilate. Other people can't determine this consciously, but pick it up subconsciously. This is one of the reasons we can tell if someone likes us. We all have the ability to tell if someone's smile is false or genuine.

The quickest way to become more charismatic is to interact with more people. Speak to people while waiting in line, or when you're out and about. Have a brief conversation with a checkout operator or server. If you find it hard to talk to people you don't know, you might start by asking people what time it is, or possibly ask for directions. You'll discover that most people will smile and be happy to help you. In some cases, you'll be able to extend the conversation, and enjoy a pleasant interaction with someone else. Every now and again, an interaction of this sort may bring you good luck.

31. Act on Your Hunches

Some people call it intuition or a sixth sense, but you don't need to believe in the metaphysical to experience hunches. A hunch is a premonition or feeling you get about something or someone. You cannot explain it logically, but something inside tells you that something is right or wrong. I've learned the hard way to act on my hunches. At times, I've allowed logic to overrule my hunches, and I've always regretted it later. Acting on my hunches gives me luck, as it tells me whether or not to proceed with a particular course of action.

32. Listen

When I was in grade school, a teacher of mine constantly told us: "You never learn anything while you're talking." I'm not sure I really understood what she meant at the time, but I've been grateful for her advice over the years. Frequently, people inadvertently give me good ideas for my books in the course of a conversation. If I'd been thinking about what to say next rather than listening, I'd have missed out on all those good ideas.

One of my most popular books, *Spirit & Dream Animals*, was written purely because I overhead two people talking about the meanings of different animals that appeared in people's dreams. I introduced myself to the two ladies, apologized for overhearing what they were talking about, and enjoyed a lengthy discussion with them on the subject. That was truly a lucky day for me.

Many people enjoy the sound of their own voice and like to dominate the conversation. I'm sure they do this because they want to be noticed, and enjoy being the center of the conversation. Maybe they want to appear smarter than everyone else. Whenever I find myself in this type of situation, I think of my old teacher's words.

When you *really* listen, you open yourself up to new ideas and experiences. You'll be able to take advantage of some of these and everyone will tell you how lucky you are.

33. Say Yes

Way back in 1967, on my first day in London, I bumped into two people I knew back home in New Zealand. They were going to a party that evening and invited me to come along. My first thought was to decline. After all, I wouldn't know anyone at the party except for the two people who'd invited me. Also, as it wasn't their party, I'd possibly be unwelcome. Despite this, I said yes, and my life changed forever. At the party, I met a young lady called Margaret, and she and I have now been married for more than forty years. If I'd turned down the opportunity, it's unlikely we'd have ever met, and both our lives would have been completely different.

Almost the same thing happened to my father when he met my mother. He had just returned home from the Second World War, and his mother had met the wife of a senior officer in my father's regiment. She invited my grandmother and father for afternoon tea. My father didn't want to go. The last thing he wanted to do was reminisce about the war with someone who had been much more senior in rank. However, his mother persisted, and he agreed to go. Serving the tea and handing around the cakes was the senior officer's niece. Less than a year later, they married. If my father had not gone to the afternoon tea—and he very nearly didn't—I would not have been born.

When you think of how your own parents and grandparents met, not to mention all the generations that preceded them, you'll realize just how lucky you are to be alive today.

We all receive invitations and opportunities that we decline for various reasons. It's impossible to say yes to everything, but before you decline, think about the possible opportunities the invitation might provide.

One of my regrets occurred about fifteen years ago in Las Vegas. I was staying with a friend. He'd just told me how tired he was when the phone rang. It was a world-famous magician who was calling to invite me to a late supper after his show. I would have loved to have gone, but because my friend had told me how tired he was, I declined and never got to meet him. It did occur to me to call a taxi, but I knew my friend would insist on driving me to the magician's hotel and back. I should have allowed my friend to drive me there, and insist on returning home by taxi. We all have regrets, but if you think carefully before saying no, chances are you'll have fewer of them.

34. Live in the Moment

The only time any of us have is now. Young children live in the present and become totally absorbed in whatever it is they are doing. Adults find this hard to do, as many people spend their time looking back to the past, and reliving problems and concerns that have no relevance to the present moment. If they're not thinking about the past, they're likely to be worried about situations and events that might occur in the future.

Life occurs in the present moment. It's hard to be lucky if you're living in the past or worrying about the future. To be truly lucky, you need to live in the present and be willing to seize the right opportunities as they present themselves.

35. Visualization

Visualization is the art of imagining the outcome you desire as clearly as you can. If, for instance, you have a job interview tomorrow morning, you might sit down comfortably, close your eyes, and imagine exactly how you want the interview to go. Maybe you'd start by visualizing yourself waking up and feeling excited about the interview. Picture yourself getting dressed, having breakfast, and going to the interview. Although you may not have been to this particular place before, you can imagine yourself sitting down and waiting to meet the person who'll be interviewing you. See yourself walking into this person's office, and then visualize the entire interview in your mind. See yourself looking confident, smiling, making good eye contact, asking questions, and giving good responses to everything the interviewer asks you. See yourself saying goodbye to the interviewer, and then imagine yourself going through the rest of your day, happy because you know you made a good impression and did everything necessary to obtain the position.

When you go to bed, visualize it all again, and tell yourself that everything will occur exactly the way you visualized it. Visualize it again on your way to the interview, and remain confident that it will work out exactly as you visualized it.

By doing this, you'll feel much more relaxed and comfortable during the actual interview. Because of this, you'll be able to think quickly during the interview, and respond to the questions in a calm, confident manner. You'll stand out from the other candidates for the position, and dramatically increase your chances of being offered the job.

Imagine the scenario if, instead of feeling relaxed and positive, you were anxious and worried about the interview. You'd probably say to yourself: "I'm feeling really nervous. Have I got the right qualifications? Will the interviewer like me? Will I make a good impression? I'm sure I'm not right for this position." Although you're not relaxing with your eyes closed while thinking these thoughts, they're still a visualization of sorts. If you go into the interview with these negative thoughts in your mind, the chances of you being offered the position are reduced enormously.

Whenever you visualize a positive outcome, your luck increases. This is partly because you'll feel confident of success, and you'll approach the situation in the right frame of mind. In addition, the universe will recognize your attitude and help you achieve your goal.

36. Be Curious

When I first started work, people constantly told me I asked too many questions. I asked because I was curious. I wanted to know why things were done in a certain way. Maybe I asked too many questions, but I learned a great deal as a result and was sometimes able to make suggestions that helped the company I worked for.

I still ask questions, but I'm not as brave as my brother-in-law. He's happy to ask the type of questions that most people won't because they're worried about appearing foolish. His curiosity has made him a fortune. People tell him he's lucky, but much of his success can be attributed to his curiosity. Asking questions and thinking about the answers has provided him with numerous opportunities he was able to capitalize on.

Ask questions. Be curious and see how lucky you become.

37. Everyone Is Important

It's impossible to know who might provide you with a lucky opportunity. You probably already treat people in authority with respect. After all, they might be able to help you directly or possibly influence people who can. However, you also need to treat less important people with the same degree of respect. Someone who is in a modest position might know someone who can help you or give you some valuable advice. Who knows what luck might come from the encounter? In the future, this person might hold a senior role and will remember how you treated him or her when you first met.

If you treat others as if they're important, they're likely to extend the same courtesy to you.

38. Make Today Special

Decide to make today a special day, a day in which nothing bothers you, and you see the best in everything that happens. You might like to make plans for your first special day a day or two ahead. Decide what you want to accomplish, who you'd like to spend the day with, and what you'd like to do. You may not be able to do this if it's a regular day at work, but you can still decide to make it your special day where everything goes well.

Once you've had one special day, you'll decide to do it again and again, until every day is a special day. When you've reached this position, you'll find nothing will bother you anymore, and you'll feel relaxed and in total control of everything that happens. You'll also find good luck occurring on a regular basis.

39. Inspire by Example

Lead your life as if you're already the person you desire to be. If you're courteous to others, speak well, smile, don't complain, and work hard, people are going to see you as a good, positive person. You must be fair, friendly, reliable, and dependable at all times. Your dress must be appropriate for whatever situation you're in. By doing all of this, you'll inspire others by your example, and this will open doors to many opportunities that might have been denied you in the past. In turn, everyone will say how lucky you are.

40. Think Win-Win

Win-win is the concept of entering into every opportunity with the object of being reasonable to everyone concerned and ensuring a positive, mutually beneficial outcome. It is based on fairness, compromise, cooperation, and mutual benefit. The traditional I-win-you-lose scenario is not a fair way of dealing with others. If you get a bigger slice of the pie, someone else gets less and will feel that you've taken advantage of them.

This doesn't mean you need to look after the other person's interests as well as your own. It does mean being honest, ethical, and treating others the way you'd like them to treat you. They need to look after their own interests while you focus on yours.

If you act honorably and sincerely toward others in all your dealings, you'll find more and more opportunities will be presented to you, demonstrating that the "pie" is actually infinite.

41. Be Adaptable

Be prepared to go with the flow. You might have your heart set on going to a particular movie. However, if it's sold out, not showing at your local cinema, or your friends don't want to see it, be willing to see a different movie, or maybe go out for dinner instead.

If you're kept waiting somewhere, don't get angry. Instead, catch up with some calls or read a book.

People who are flexible and adaptable have much more fun than people who are rigid, dogmatic, and set in their ways. If you're open-minded, listen to new ideas, and change your plans when necessary, you'll achieve much more success and happiness than the dinosaurs who won't adapt. You'll also be luckier in every way.

42. Help Others

You can help others in many different ways. One of the best ways to help someone is to spend time with them. Even a smile will help. Helping others makes you feel good about yourself. It involves interacting with another human being and there's no knowing where that might lead. It could even result in a lifelong friendship. It also improves the life of someone else, and this makes the world a better place for everyone.

43. Find a Mentor

Mentors frequently appear in people's lives at just the right moment. Warren Buffett, who has himself mentored many others, was mentored by Benjamin Graham. Ray Charles had Wiley Pittman. In both cases, the mentor arrived at exactly the right moment for the person being mentored.

Mentors can increase your luck in many ways. They can teach you valuable skills and techniques. They can introduce you to influential people who might open doors for you. They can provide opportunities to learn and practice your skills. They provide encouragement, and act as sounding boards to your ideas. Quite apart from anything else, a mentor will have your best interests at heart, and will become a good friend you can call upon for help and advice at any time.

Mentors may stay connected with you for decades. Some stay with you long enough to get you started and then move on. Although I wasn't aware of it at the time, some of the teachers I had at school were also mentors. They were able to see potentials in me I hadn't yet recognized, and gently nudged me in the right direction. These were all short-term mentors, but they were no less valuable than long-term mentors.

Mentors will usually find you, but there's no reason you can't seek a mentor if you're ready for one. Seek out people in the field you want to succeed in, and find someone knowledgeable and easy to get along with. Ask this person if you can contact him or her for advice every now and again. Most people will feel flattered to be asked, and gradually that person will become your mentor. Of course, not everyone wants to fulfill that role. If you get turned down, simply go through the process again and again until you find your mentor.

44. Be a Mentor

Many people who have been mentored ultimately become mentors themselves. There's a special joy in passing on information and helping people who are ready to receive it. Mentoring others also increases your luck. Often the person you're mentoring will be younger than you, and he or she will provide you with the viewpoint and attitudes of a different generation. This provides you with additional opportunities you might not have seen otherwise. The satisfaction and pleasure you receive from mentoring a person with potential will increase your self-esteem. By helping someone else, you're benefiting the whole world, albeit in a small way, and the universe will reward you. When you work in harmony with the universe, you can't help but be lucky.

45. Practice the Golden Rule

"Do unto others as you would have them do unto you." The world's main spiritual traditions teach the concept of treating other people the way we would like to be treated ourselves. This maxim predates Christianity by thousands of years. In *The Eloquent Peasant*, a popular story during the time of the Middle Kingdom (c. 2040–c. 1650 BCE) in ancient Egypt, are the words: "Now this is the command: Do to the doer to cause that he do thus to you."[10]

The golden rule is not always easy in practice, as everyone has to deal with difficult people from time to time. However, it is in these situations that you most need to practice it.

When you practice the golden rule, you'll think about the effect your actions have on others, and be able to see yourself in the other person's position. In other words, you'll be empathizing with them. By treating others with compassion, kindness, and respect, you'll feel differently about yourself. People will respond and trust you in return. You'll also receive opportunities you may not have been presented with otherwise.

46. Feel Lucky

Feeling lucky is closely related to attitude. If you go through life expecting fortuitous and lucky events to occur, they probably will. You'll also recognize them when they appear. Conversely, if you go through life with a pessimistic attitude, you'll miss out on lucky opportunities as you'll be focused on the negative aspects of everything you experience.

Lucky people create their own luck because they have a positive attitude toward life, and expect good outcomes. They experience just as many ups and downs as everyone else, but because they expect to be lucky, they pick themselves up again and start looking for the next opportunity.

47. Self-Respect

We're all harder on ourselves than we are on others. You're not likely to tell a friend that he or she is lazy or stupid, but you may well say these things to yourself. You deserve all the respect you naturally give to others. Start appreciating yourself for the wonderful creation you are. In the entire history of the world, there has never been another person exactly like you. You are unique and special.

Be honest with yourself, too. We all make mistakes. When you do, admit it, learn from the experience, and move on. I know several people who constantly blame past partners for everything that is wrong in their lives. It would be interesting to know what their previous partners have to say about this. Almost always, there are mistakes on both sides. Admit your mistakes, forgive others and yourself, and move on.

Part of the process is to avoid people who don't give you the respect you deserve. They cause unnecessary stress and undermine your self-esteem.

When you respect yourself, you're able to face every situation calmly. You'll be open to good opportunities, and this will increase your luck.

48. It's Never Too Late

You can change your life at any age. You can start attracting luck at twenty, fifty, or eighty-five years of age. Your physical age has nothing to do with it. It is never too late.

Many years ago, a sales-representative friend of mine told me he felt he was getting old, as most people in his industry were under forty. He was thirty-eight at the time, and thought it was too late to start again. I thought it strange that someone under forty would think that way, but since then I've met many people who also felt trapped by their ages. My friend enjoyed playing poker. After a great deal of encouragement from his friends, he placed a small advertisement in a local paper offering to teach others how to improve their game. This new venture started modestly, but now he's making a full-time living from it, and feels happy and fulfilled.

There are numerous examples of people starting a new career in their forties, fifties, and later. Grandma Moses (1860–1961), who started painting in her seventies, is a classic example. In 2006, one of her paintings, *Sugaring Off*, sold for $1.2 million.

A retired man in my city opened up a store selling fresh fruit and vegetables when he was sixty-seven. Now, fifteen years later, he runs a thriving empire of stores offering fresh fruit and vegetables at reasonable prices. I'm sure he has no intention of ever retiring.

Julia Child started out as an advertising copywriter. She was almost fifty when her book, *Mastering the Art of French Cooking*, was published and the career that made her famous began.

Maturity can be an advantage in many fields, as you'll have many years of life experience behind you. If you're concerned about your age, spend time evaluating your skills and interests, and decide which one, or more, you'd like to pursue. I can guarantee that as soon as you start, more and more opportunities will come your way, and people will start calling you "lucky."

49. Life Is a Journey

Every year I set goals for myself. I find them helpful in keeping me on track, and I'm sure I've accomplished more with them than I would have without them. However, I consider my goals to be guides, and have no hesitation in changing or even discarding goals, if circumstances change or a fresh opportunity opens up. My goals are flexible, and it's not the end of the world if I fail to achieve them.

Many people become trapped by their goals. They remain totally fixated on them, and as a result, suffer stress, anxiety, and uncertainty when they remain elusive, or they feel they're not progressing as quickly as they'd like. It's hard to feel lucky when you're constantly stressed, pressured, and worried.

A better, and easier, approach is to see life as a journey, rather than a destination. By focusing on the journey, you'll be able to appreciate the ride and will spend most of your time enjoying the present moment, rather than worrying about what might or might not eventuate in the future. This approach opens you up to luck in all its forms. Many serendipitous moments, for example, will occur when you're enjoying the present and are open to fresh experiences.

50. Choose Your Direction

Every day you make choices and decisions. Admittedly, most of these are minor, but they demonstrate your ability to evaluate and make choices in every area of your life. You have the power to choose the direction of your life. In fact, you're creating it every day with the choices and decisions you make. You can change your thoughts, your reactions, and even your feelings about any aspect of your life. If you're not happy with the way your life is going, you can't call yourself a lucky person. However, by deliberately making different choices, you have the ability to change your present and your future, and this enables luck to enter into your life again.

51. Values Plus Goals

To be lucky, your values and goals need to be aligned. If they're not, luck is unlikely to shine on you, and you'll feel tense or lacking in motivation. If your values are high but your goals are low, you'll find it hard to motivate yourself to achieve them. If your goals are high but your values are low, you'll experience little satisfaction in accomplishing them.

When your values and goals are aligned, you'll feel positive, motivated—and lucky.

52. Eliminate Negative Habits

A friend of mine is always late. He arrives late for appointments, meetings, and social events. He's missed flights, and was even too late on one occasion to meet the person he most admires. This was just one of countless opportunities he's lost. As well as costing him opportunities, this bad habit has caused him a great deal of unnecessary stress.

He's not alone. We all have negative habits that cost us opportunities, create stress, and slow down our progress through life. If you want to increase your luck, you need to overcome these bad habits.

Choose one negative habit, and focus on it for a month. Congratulate yourself each time you overcome it, but don't beat yourself down when you fail. Simply remind yourself of your reasons for eliminating this behavior, and resolve to do better next time. Psychologists claim that habits can be changed in just twenty-eight days. Consequently, approximately a month after you decide to overcome an undesirable habit, you should be well on the way to success. Allow another month to ensure the new behavior has become your normal way of life, and then tackle another bad habit. As you do this, your luck will increase.

53. Accept Yourself

You can change negative habits, but you can't turn yourself into someone you don't want to be. If you're an extrovert, for instance, you can learn to listen more or to stop constantly striving to be the center of attention. However, you shouldn't try to become an introvert, as that is not who you are. Likewise, if you're an introvert, you should try to be more outgoing and to speak more, but you shouldn't aim to become an extrovert. No matter if you're an introvert, extrovert, or somewhere in between, you should seek your own particular strengths and work with them. You're most likely to be lucky when you're making the most of your natural talents and abilities.

54. Be Kind

Surprise someone with an act of kindness. If whoever is behind you in line at the supermarket has only one or two items and you have a cart full of groceries, let the person ahead of you. You'll feel good, the person you let in front of you will be grateful, and for a while the world will be a better place for both of you. Even something as simple as a smile or a friendly word can help others.

Being kind doesn't necessarily cost anything, but it helps everyone involved, and makes you feel good about yourself. Your luck cannot help but increase with so much positive energy around you.

55. The Energy of Drishti

Drishti is a Sanskrit word that relates to using the eyes to focus attention on something specific for a particular purpose. In yoga, it's used to focus on one of nine specific points while the person meditates or practices different asanas. We all use our eyes to see, but yogis also use their eyes to perceive an inner reality that is not normally visible. It enables them to see the divine in everything.

You can practice drishti by using your eyes to send positive, compassionate, and kindly energy to everyone you come across in your everyday life: family, friends, acquaintances, and strangers alike. They may not know you're practicing drishti, but they'll sense your benevolence, love, and care. You'll experience luck everywhere you go as a result.

56. Spend Time with a Child

Ask a teacher if there's any truth in the saying "kids say the darndest things," and you'll immediately be told several humorous stories about life from a child's point of view. Children look at the world differently than adults, and you can learn a great deal by listening to them and thinking about what they say. It's a privilege to temporarily see the world through a child's eyes. You'll be amazed at the amount of wisdom a small child has and how deeply they think about what's going on in their lives.

Because of this, I always feel lucky whenever I'm with my grandchildren, especially one-on-one. Although they can be hard work at times, I always return home feeling revitalized and full of ideas.

57. Change One Thing

People often become frustrated when they try to change everything about their lives with one massive effort. It can't be done. However, you can make huge changes in your life if you make one small change, followed by another, and then another. By making a series of small changes, you'll ultimately experience huge benefits. It takes three to four weeks to change a habit. Allow as much time as necessary for the habit change to occur, as some changes take more work and effort than others.

There's another benefit you'll gain from making a series of incremental changes. Each small success will make you feel better about yourself. This will be reflected in your posture, facial expressions, and thoughts. You'll feel good about yourself and will become luckier with each change you make.

58. Get in the Zone

When you're in what athletes call "the zone," you become so involved in what you're doing that you lose track of time. The task you're engaged in should require your full involvement and be both challenging and enjoyable. People often find themselves in the zone when they're participating in a sport, playing music, writing in a diary, meditating, or doing yoga. An acquaintance of mine is a cabinet maker who appears to go into a trance when he's working on a major project. He finds it easy to enter the zone. I find myself in the zone frequently when I'm writing. Much to my family's amazement, I can sometimes forget to eat lunch when my writing is going well.

You're especially lucky whenever you're in the zone, as you're gaining pleasure and satisfaction from working on and completing a difficult or demanding task.

59. Random Acts of Kindness

Most of the time, it's a pleasure to help friends and family members. We do this when someone we know has done something good for us, or because we want to express our love in a tangible way.

However, there's also a special joy that comes from helping complete strangers for no reason at all. Practicing random acts of kindness can become addictive, as it's so beneficial for everyone involved. Even the smallest gesture has the power to change a life. I started practicing random acts of kindness when someone saved me from getting a parking ticket by putting some coins into a parking meter. I have no idea who that person was, but more than twenty years later, I still remember it and try to pay back his or her good deed by doing similar things for others. A friend of one of my sons regularly puts additional money into vending machines, so the next person will receive a free snack.

Of course, you can also do this without spending any money. Paying someone a compliment costs nothing and makes everyone feel good. Simply smiling at someone can raise their spirits. A retired man I know spends a few hours a week visiting people in a retirement village. He raises the spirits of many lonely people there. An elderly lady I know regularly receives home-grown vegetables from a young man who lives on her street. He enjoys gardening and gains pleasure from giving his excess vegetables to people within walking distance of his home. Donating time to a worthy cause is a particularly good way to help your local community.

Practicing random acts of kindness increases your luck in many ways. A basic law of the universe says that if you do a good deed for someone, sooner or later you'll receive something good in return. Sometimes you'll meet the people you're helping. These new contacts may become friends who open up new opportunities for you. Your life will improve, as helping others is a guaranteed way of increasing your happiness.

— Part Two —

Lucky Tools

Throughout history, people have sought ways to attract good luck. These include words, phrases, gemstones, and charms. Even today, some people believe that saying the right words, or wearing the right gemstone or charm, will attract good luck. In fact, this may well work for them, as their belief in the power of whatever it is they're using will keep them focused on their desire.

I have a large collection of lucky charms I've collected over the years. I don't believe they'll attract good luck to me; however, when I carry one with me, it makes me think about the concept of luck, and how lucky I am. It also encourages me to maintain a positive attitude everywhere I go. Because I feel lucky and positive, good things tend to occur.

Consequently, a lucky tool works whether or not you believe in it. Select one or two items from this section, and experiment with them.

Let's assume you've chosen Number 105: Buttons. It doesn't matter where the button came from. Place it in a pocket, or somewhere else where you'll see or feel it several times a day. Every time you become aware of the button, touch, stroke, or hold it and remind yourself how lucky you are. If necessary, spend a moment thinking about the most important blessings in your life, such as family, friends, and life itself. This simple act will make you feel lucky, and because you'll be expecting good things to happen, they will.

Three

Lucky Words and Phrases

Introduction

Throughout history, certain words have been considered powerful and have been used as charms to attract good luck. Originally, charms were words that were either spoken or sung. The word "charm" is derived from the French word *charme*, which means "song." A good example of a charm of this sort is the blessing that a priest gives at the end of a church service. Once people started writing words down, charms became associated with amulets and talismans, which are physical objects. However, the power of certain words has always remained.

A close friend of mine makes his living as a magician but is also a keen gambler. Whenever he enters a casino, he says to himself, "Abracadabra!" He considers this to be a lucky word as it's used by magicians as a magic spell, as well as people such as gamblers who need extra luck for a specific purpose.

You may find one of the words in this section resonates with you for some reason. You might like the sound of it or enjoy reading about it. You might decide to use it because you haven't heard of it before. I used the word *nefer* for a while after someone introduced me to the word. No matter what the reason might be, try using it whenever you need some additional help, or luck, in whatever it is you are doing. You don't have to believe the word itself possesses lucky properties. When you repeat the word to yourself, you remind yourself of the concept of luck, which will make you more receptive to any potential lucky opportunities.

60. Abracadabra

Abracadabra has a long history, and its origins are lost in the mists of time. The word was first written down by the Roman physician Quintus Serenus Sammonicus in 208 CE, but it is believed to be much older than that. It may be derived from the Chaldean phrase *abbada ke dabra*, which means "Perish like the word."[1]

The talisman for abracadabra consists of eleven lines. The top row contains the word abracadabra, the second line eliminates the final letter, and a letter is dropped in each row until the bottom row contains one letter—an A.

ABRACADABRA
ABRACADABR
ABRACADAB
ABRACADA
ABRACAD
ABRACA
ABRAC
ABRA
AB
A

This figure creates a funnel that produces powerful energy that defeats any form of evil. During the Middle Ages, it was worn around the neck as an amulet to ward off illness. Many years ago, I walked across a beach at dusk and found someone had drawn this talisman in the sand. I hope it provided that person with good luck.

Although the word *abracadabra* is commonly used nowadays by children's entertainers, it has not lost its power and can be said any time you desire powerful magic in your life. It is a potent spoken lucky charm.

61. Kuwabara

Kuwabara is a Japanese word that people used when calling on the gods in ancient times. The word was originally the name of a village. When a thunder god fell from the clouds, a young girl in the village helped him return to the sky. The god thanked her and said that because of what she had done, lightning would never harm the village.

Japanese people say, "Kuwabara, kuwabara" in the same way that Western people say, "knock on wood." It wards off bad luck and encourages good luck.

62. Bedooh

The word *bedooh* is considered a magical word in parts of the Middle East, Turkey, and Iran. It comes from an Arabian word meaning "he has walked well." It can be inscribed on seals, gems, swords, and helmets to create a protective amulet that also brings luck. The Sufi writer Ahmad ibn Ali al-Buni (d. 1225) wrote: "Whoever carries this word engraved on a ruby mounted in gold is sure of constant good fortune." [2]

63. Mahurat

Mahurat is a Hindi word that means "a lucky moment," usually when a venture is just begun. In Bollywood, Indian filmmakers call the day when a projected new film is announced a Mahurat Day.

Special days, such as weddings, baptisms, naming ceremonies, moving into a new home, and starting a new job, are Mahurat Days. In India, farmers call the days on which important activities, such as sowing or reaping, are started, Mahurat Days.

You can have your own special Mahurat Day whenever you wish.

64. Prosit

Prosit, or *Prost*, is a popular toast in Germany and Scandinavia. It means "may it benefit," and is a wish of good health and good luck. "Good luck" is also frequently used as a toast.

65. Handsel

A *handsel* is a small gift or token given to someone to wish them good luck. It can also mean the first payment someone receives in a series of payments. This could be the first pay someone receives in a new job, the first sale made in a new business, or the first gift someone receives on his or her birthday. The word *handsel* is derived from an Old Norse word meaning "legal transfer."

66. Fu

Fu or *Hu* is the Chinese word for good luck. Strictly speaking, it means "good luck comes." At the time of the Chinese New Year, thousands of posters of this word are displayed, with the character for *fu* printed upside-down. This is because the Chinese word for "upside down" sounds the same as the word for "comes."

67. Nefer

The ancient Egyptians had a number of different meanings for the word *nefer*. They were all positive and included goodness, perfection, beauty, and good luck. Queen Nefertiti was named after this word, and the most famous depiction of her shows her wearing a necklace of golden nefer beads. The hieroglyph for nefer looked similar to an upright lute, and nefer beads were carved in the same shape. People who could afford them wore small red gemstones carved into the shape of nefers around their wrists and necks as lucky charms.

68. Mazel Tov

Mazel tov is a Hebrew phrase that means "good luck." It is not a wish for good luck, but recognizes that good luck has occurred. Saying "Mazel tov" to someone is therefore similar to saying, "Lucky you!"

The Mishnaic Hebrew word *mazzal* means "constellation of stars." This relates the phrase *mazel tov* to the idea of being born under a lucky star, or possibly a good constellation of stars.

69. Namaste

Namaste is derived from two ancient Sanskrit words that mean "bow to you." It is a traditional Indian greeting that involves holding both hands pressed together with the fingers pointing upwards in front of the chest, while bowing slightly and saying, "Namaste." It indicates deep respect you feel for the other person. Because it involves no physical contact, it can be used when meeting people of different status or gender.

70. Happy Birthday

You should wish people "happy birthday" as early in the morning as possible on the day of their birthday. This brings good luck to both you and the person having the birthday. You should offer this wish to children as soon as they wake up. This provides the child with protection as well as good luck.

The tradition of saying "happy birthday" is extremely old, and was originally said to protect the person from evil spirits who might be attracted to the birthday celebration. Evil spirits were also thought to be especially dangerous at times of change, making a birthday a double opportunity for spirits to wreak harm on the person celebrating the birthday.

Four

....

Lucky Crystals and Gemstones

Introduction

Many crystals and gemstones are sought after for their beauty, but through-out history people have also treasured them for their mystical properties. In fact, many scholars believe ancient people originally wore gems as amulets and charms rather than for mere adornment. All crystals and gemstones contain energy, and some are believed to bring luck to whoever owns them.

You can use your "lucky" gemstones in a number of different ways. You might display several in a small container on your desk. You can pick them up and fondle them whenever you feel the need for additional help or good luck. You may choose a particular gem and wear it as a ring, bracelet, or necklace, or possibly carry it with you in a pocket or purse. Touch, hold, or fondle it whenever necessary.

I enjoy carrying a gemstone in my pocket as a lucky charm. I like the feel of it in my hand, and handling it reminds me how lucky I am. If I don't happen to have a gemstone with me, I find it almost as helpful to imag-ine that I'm carrying a gemstone in my pocket. This imaginary gemstone provides me with protection, harmony, and the ability to stand up for myself no matter what occurs. Because of this, I feel confident, stress free, and lucky all day long.

If you'd like to try carrying a gemstone or crystal as a lucky charm, choose the most attractive stone you can. Keep it in a pocket or purse and handle it from time to time during the day. Each time you do this, remind yourself that you're carrying it as a lucky charm. This will make you think of luck, and because of that, good opportunities will come your way.

Here are some of the more important lucky stones, with their traditional "lucky" meanings.

71. Agate

Agate is a variety of quartz that can be found in a variety of colors, including white, gray, orange, blue, red, black, and banded. It has been used in jewelry since Babylonian times. It is considered lucky, as it provides strength and protection. It provides acceptance and the strength to carry on no matter what has occurred.

72. Alexandrite

Legend says that this stone was named after the heir to the throne of Russia, Alexander II, as it was discovered on his twenty-first birthday (April 29, 1839). Alexandrite is an unusual stone as it is green in daylight, but changes to light red in artificial light. People wear it to attract both love and good luck.

73. Amazonite

Amazonite is a semiopaque blue-green crystal found mainly in Russia. It helps you set worthwhile goals and provides the motivation to enable you to achieve them.

74. Amethyst

Amethyst is a violet stone that was used by the ancient Greeks as a cure for drunkenness. It's a powerful stone that relieves headaches, promotes a good night's sleep, and encourages spirituality and wisdom. As amethyst also increases intuition, it's considered a stone that will increase your luck in every way.

75. Aquamarine

Aquamarine is a blue-green gemstone that helps eliminate stress and worry. It is found in many parts of the world, but the best quality ones come from Brazil. It provides peace of mind, happiness, and courage.

76. Aventurine

Aventurine is a quartzite found in several colors, including yellow, green, blue, and red. It is considered a stone of chance and luck. Consequently, it is the favorite stone of gamblers. It also calms the emotions and has a stabilizing effect on the body.

77. Carnelian

Carnelian is a reddish-brown gemstone found in India and South America. It provides physical energy when required. It is considered lucky for anyone engaged in athletic pursuits. It also provides inner strength and a sense of humor. Napoleon had a carnelian attached to his watch chain as a protective amulet.

78. Cat's-Eye

Cat's-eye is a gemstone that when cut in a convex form reveals a luminous band that looks like the eye of a cat. Cat's-eye helps you accept and understand others. It provides insight, protection, and good luck. It also enhances determination, persistence, and large ambitions.

79. Citrine

Citrine is a yellow, orange, or gold member of the quartz family. It enhances the mind and is considered lucky for people involved in business. It should be kept in the cash drawer or wherever money is stored on the premises. It can also be worn or carried on the person to attract good luck in all financial undertakings. It is sometimes known as the "merchant's stone" or the "money stone" because of its alleged ability to attract money.

80. Diamond

Diamond is a transparent form of pure carbon and the hardest surface known. Diamonds are the "king of gems," and have been considered the universal symbol of love for many years. Diamonds are also useful for people involved in business, as they attract luck in all financial dealings. This may explain why many successful businesspeople wear diamond rings and jewelry.

81. Emerald

The emerald is a bright green beryl. It was sacred to the goddess Venus and has always been associated with love. Consequently, it's a popular stone to give to a lover, to ensure the relationship is long-lasting and happy. The emerald also soothes troubled minds and attracts prosperity.

82. Garnet

Garnets can be found in many colors but are predominantly red. They provide good luck for people in business and those following a standard career path. If your career is not progressing as smoothly or as quickly as you'd like, keep a few garnets in a small container on your desk. Garnets also bolster confidence and self-esteem.

83. Hematite

Hematite is the mineral version of iron oxide. It is usually a steely gray in color, but can also be black, brown, or brownish-red. It is sometimes known as the "stone that bleeds" as it gains a reddish streak when rubbed against a test surface. Hematite provides courage and motivation, and it enables you to understand the motives and actions of others. Hematite is the perfect stone if you need more luck in your marriage or relationships.

84. Jade

Jade is arguably *the* stone associated with luck. Greenstone, or green jade, has always been treasured by the Maori people of New Zealand because it brings good luck. Beautifully carved jade charms are passed down through the family or buried with the owner.

In India, only royalty was allowed to own jade because it was considered so powerful. Commoners who dared to own some were put to death.

In China, jade has been treasured for more than four thousand years, and is often worn to provide protection and attract good luck. Jade symbolizes constancy, nobility, and immortality. In the past, newborn babies were presented with jade bangles to ward off bad luck. If the bangle remained intact, the child would always enjoy good luck. Jade butterflies are believed to bestow good luck in love. Consequently, a newly engaged man will sometimes give his fiancée a jade butterfly to wear.

85. Red Jasper

Jasper is a form of chalcedony and is usually red, yellow, brown, or green. Red jasper eliminates stress and anxiety and acts as a powerful protective stone. It provides courage, independence, and feelings of personal security. It eases stress and promotes a good night's sleep. It's considered a lucky stone for anyone who performs in front of the public.

86. Lodestone

Magnetite, or lodestone, is magnetic iron ore. It's been considered lucky for at least four thousand years. Pliny the Elder wrote that it was discovered by a Greek shepherd named Magnes who found that it stuck to the nails in his shoes. Alexander the Great issued lodestones to his soldiers as lucky charms.

Because magnetite attracts iron, lodestone became associated with love, as it simulated the attraction two lovers have for each other. People wore it to attract the right partner. In Chinese, lodestone is called *t'su shi*, which means "the loving stone."

Men can increase their strength, courage, virility, and good luck by wearing or carrying a piece of magnetite. However, women are not supposed to wear magnetite at any time.

87. Malachite

Malachite is a copper ore that contains patterns of both light and dark green. Six thousand years ago, the ancient Egyptians mined malachite to create amulets and charms. As they believed malachite protected young children, they were frequently attached to cradles to protect sleeping babies.

In the Middle Ages, people wore malachite for protection. They believed the stone would break into pieces at the first sign of danger, and this would give them enough time to escape, or to face up to the danger.

Malachite has been called the "salesperson's stone" as it is reputed to provide salespeople with confidence, protection, astuteness, and the ability to sell. Consequently, many salespeople wear it to attract good luck.

Today it is one of the most popular stones for use in lucky charms.

88. Moonstone

The moonstone is sacred in India and is believed to provide good luck to everyone who wears it. It is also a popular gift for lovers, as it arouses the passions and enables couples to think about their future lives together.

The moonstone has been associated with the lunar cycle since Roman times, making it a popular amulet and charm for women.

The expression "once in a blue moon" comes from the moonstone. In India, people believe that every twenty-one years the sun and moon create a special juxtaposition with each other, and whenever this occurs, blue moonstones can be found on the seashore. The moonstone has always been a popular stone with people who are seeking good luck.

89. Quartz

Quartz is one of the most commonly found minerals around the world. Large quartz crystals have been found in the Egyptian Temple of Luxor, showing that mankind has been using it for at least eight thousand years. It was custom in ancient Greece to hold a piece of quartz while praying. People believed their prayers would be answered if they did this.

Clear quartz provides energy and stamina. Rose quartz is pale pink in color, and is said to attract loyalty, love, and fertility. Clear and rose quartz are the varieties used most often to attract good luck.

90. Smoky Quartz

Smoky quartz is a form of silicon dioxide. It varies in color from brown to black. Its smoky appearance is caused by free silicon. Smoky quartz is believed to keep one's feet firmly on the ground. It encourages creativity, happiness, and a positive approach to life. It provides strength, endurance, and determination. This makes it a highly positive and motivating stone for athletes.

91. Ruby

Ruby is the legendary stone of India. Statues of Buddha usually have a small red ruby on the forehead, as red symbolizes his reincarnation. Early Christians considered ruby to be the most valuable stone of all. They believed that God ordered Aaron to wear a ruby on his neck. Aaron also had a ruby in his breastplate of gems.

Ruby has always been considered a positive and happy stone. In fact, the more rubies you possess, the happier you should be. In addition, you'll always have plenty of good luck.

92. Sodalite

Sodalite is a royal blue gemstone found in Greenland and northern Canada. It contains small traces of white calcite. Sodalite is said to calm the mind, eliminate worries, and provide inner peace. It is considered a lucky stone for writers and anyone involved in any form of communication.

93. Tiger's-Eye

Tiger's-Eye is sometimes known as the "stone of independence," as it provides confidence and self-assurance. In some parts of the world, it is used to provide protection against the evil eye. In most places, though, it's used to attract good luck. Because of its associations with both independence and good luck, tiger's-eye is said to be particularly useful for entrepreneurs and people with big dreams.

94. Tourmaline

Tourmaline is found in most parts of the world. It is sometimes known as the "gemstone of the rainbow," as it can be found in all the colors of the rainbow. Some tourmalines even change color when moved from natural to artificial light. As some tourmalines contain two colors, tourmalines provide additional—double—luck when needed.

Black tourmaline removes negativity and provides happiness and good luck. Green tourmaline attracts worldly success. Pink tourmaline attracts love as well as friends.

95. Turquoise

Turquoise is the most popular amulet stone in the world, and has been used to provide good luck for thousands of years. It's a popular stone for lovers, and is said to lose its color if the love fades. It's also said to do this if your luck or health are threatened. If this occurs, the remedy is to replace your turquoise with one that is brighter in color.

In Arab countries, many horses wear turquoise amulets to protect both the horse and rider. This tradition probably began in ancient Persia. As horses were thought to pull the sun through the heavens and turquoise reminded people of the sky, it naturally became a good luck amulet. In Turkey, turquoise is called *fayruz*, which can be interpreted as "stone of happiness" or "lucky stone."

In the Middle East, turquoise averts the malevolent glances of the evil eye, and in Tibet it is used to provide protection for statues of religious figures.

As turquoise is believed to attract love, happiness, and prosperity, it's no wonder it's called the "lucky stone."

96. Birthstones

The belief that there is a special stone for each month of the year can be found in *Antiquities of the Jews* by the first-century Jewish historian Flavius Josephus. He related the twelve gemstones in biblical Aaron's breastplate to the months of the year. However, the tradition of actually wearing the gemstone that relates to the person's month of birth dates back only as far as eighteenth century Poland.[1] It is said to be lucky to possess the gemstone that relates to your month of birth. The particular stones have changed over the years, and the current "standard" listing bears little resemblance to the breastplate gemstones.

Here is the list issued by the Jewelry Industry Council in America in 1952:

+ January—Garnet (constancy)

+ February—Amethyst (sincerity)

+ March—Aquamarine (foresight) or bloodstone (courage)

+ April—Diamond (innocence)

+ May—Emerald (happiness in love)

+ June—Pearl (purity), moonstone (passion), or alexandrite (luck)

+ July—Ruby (purity)

+ August—Peridot (beauty) or sardonyx (happy marriage)

+ September—Sapphire (love)

+ October—Opal (hope) or pink tourmaline (love)

+ November—Topaz (fidelity) or citrine (clarity of thought)

+ December—Turquoise (prosperity) or zircon (success)

The British Goldsmiths' list is almost the same, but did not include alexandrite (June), pink tourmaline (October), or zircon (December). They also have two gemstones that do not appear on the Jewelry Industry Council's list: rock crystal for April and lapis lazuli for September.

Five

....

Lucky Charms

Introduction

Throughout history, people have carried lucky charms and amulets to attract good luck and to ward off bad luck. It's fascinating how powerful a charm you can touch or hold can be.

A few years ago, my then seven-year-old granddaughter suffered from anxiety whenever she was away from home. My daughter made her a small stuffed heart-shaped charm to hold whenever she felt any sign of insecurity. It was about two inches long, and the fabric contained her favorite colors. My daughter told Ava that whenever she held or touched it, it would remind her that all her family loved her. This little charm worked amazingly well, and all signs of anxiety disappeared in a matter of weeks.

I have a lucky acorn that sits beside my computer. Whenever I find it hard to write, I hold it and think of the moment when Ava gave it to me when she was four years old. When I put the acorn back, I'm able to start writing again.

Do I really believe that this acorn gives me luck? Belief is not necessary. The acorn works because it brings back happy memories, and makes me feel good. Because I'm feeling positive and upbeat, I also feel lucky.

Many sports teams have a mascot because they hope it will attract good luck. The word "mascot" is derived from the French word *masco*, which means "sorceress." The sorceress repels evil spirits and other forms of negativity. Anything can be used as a mascot. In effect, a mascot is a lucky charm that is intended to bring good luck to a group, rather than an individual.

Lucky charms work because of the belief the owners have in them. Although they believe in the efficacy of their charms, these people are also likely to believe their thoughts and actions create the events in their lives. They know at least subconsciously that worry and uncertainty can lead to accidents and disappointment while confidence and a positive attitude are frequently indicators of success.

Lucky charms help many people maintain a more positive outlook on life, enabling them to become luckier than they were before.

Although some people consider lucky charms to be nothing more than superstition, a recent study by researchers at the University of Cologne found that lucky charms improve people's memory, performance, and confidence.[1]

You can use almost anything as a lucky charm. A friend of mine always carries a lucky coin in his pocket. I know he takes it seriously, even though he jokes that any coin in his possession is a lucky coin. When I carry a coin for luck, I usually prefer to carry a coin that I've picked up during an overseas trip, rather than a coin of the currency of the country I'm living in. However, a local coin will work well, especially if you can find one that was minted in the year of your birth. It's best to keep your lucky coin separate from any loose change you may have. During the day, whenever you have a few spare moments, fondle the coin and thank it for bringing you good luck.

97. Acorn

In Norse mythology the oak tree is considered sacred. The ancient Druids were said to wear acorns to attract good luck. Because the tiny acorn transforms itself into a mighty oak tree, it symbolizes vigor, power, and longevity, as well as good luck.

98. Ankh

The ankh is an ancient Egyptian cross that symbolizes life. It is a T-shaped cross with an oval loop on the top. Pharaohs were often depicted holding an ankh. The ankh provides protection as well as good luck.

Most people who wear an ankh carry it on a chain around their neck. If you do this, you should touch it whenever you become aware of it, and tell yourself how lucky you are.

99. Badger's Tooth

In the nineteenth century, gamblers often sewed a badger's tooth in the right-hand pocket of their waistcoats to provide them with good luck when playing cards. I thought this was an old, outmoded idea until a few months ago when I saw someone handling one in the lobby of a casino in Phoenix.

100. Bee

Bees were considered sacred by the ancient Babylonians, Egyptians, and Greeks, and have always been symbols of good luck. It's an indication of good fortune coming up if a bee flies into your home and then leaves. If a bee flies into your home and appears reluctant to leave, it's a sign that a visitor is coming to see you. However, it's a sign of bad luck if a bee dies inside your home. Wearing a charm in the shape of a bee should increase your popularity and provide you with good luck.

101. Bird

A charm in the shape of a bird will increase your energy, happiness, and potential for good luck. Birds have always been considered messengers who convey messages between heaven and earth. Because of this, a bird charm should also improve your communication skills.

102. Blue

Blue has always been considered a lucky color. This is because people in the past believed heaven was up in the sky, and as the sky was blue, that must be God's favorite color. Consequently, even today, some people wear blue beads because they believe this color is a sign of good luck and will ward off all forms of negativity. An old saying goes: "Touch blue and your wish will come true."

The tradition of wearing something blue to attract good luck goes back about a century and a half. Brides traditionally wear something blue, but in the late nineteenth-century men wore blue stocking supporters, women wore blue beads, and children wore blue ribbons around their necks. This was all done to attract good luck.[2] If you need more luck, you should wear something blue. Think of your desire for good luck every time you happen to notice the blue item of clothing.

103. Buckeye

Buckeyes, or horse chestnuts, are beautiful, brown, silky nuts that are flat on one side and rounded on the other. They are called buckeyes because of a circular mark on the flat side that looks approximately like the eye of a deer.

In many parts of the world, people carry a buckeye with them as a good luck charm. When I was a child, I walked to school and passed a horse chestnut tree every day. I was extremely popular at school whenever the tree shed its nuts, as everyone wanted one because they liked the feel of them in their hand.

This must be one of the reasons the humble buckeye became a good luck charm. People probably picked them up, liked the feel of them, and kept them. Because I've had a lifelong connection with buckeyes, it's probably my favorite good luck charm. Unlike normal chestnuts, buckeyes are inedible.

See also CHESTNUTS.

104. Butterfly

A butterfly charm will increase your sense of fun and *joie de vivre*, as well as provide good luck. Butterflies also symbolize freedom, good health, and happiness. It's always been considered a sign of good luck if a white butterfly settles on or near you.

105. Buttons

Buttons are said to be especially lucky if found by chance. They're also lucky if given as a gift from a friend, as they symbolize lifelong friendship. A shiny button attracts new friends. A single button, especially one that has been given to you, makes a perfect good luck charm. A jar full of buttons also serves the same purpose. The container can be shaken whenever you need good luck. My grandmother had a metal tin full of buttons, and as children my brother, sisters, and I loved shaking it for luck. Some people make good-luck bracelets from buttons they have been given. This not only gives them good luck, but also ensures the wearer's friendship with the person or people who gave them the buttons will remain intact.

It's important to put each button into its correct buttonhole when you're getting dressed. It's bad luck if you fail to do this, but you can remedy the situation by taking the garment off completely and starting again.

106. Cameo

Cameos are medallions or brooches containing a profile of a head, or a scene, on the face. Cameos are generally made from a hard stone, such as onyx, and are carved in relief against a background of a different color. A cameo needs to be owned and loved for seven years before it becomes a lucky charm. They frequently become family heirlooms that are passed down from generation to generation. Cameos provide good luck and happiness for the wearer, and the good luck carries on to each new generation, as long as the cameo remains in the family.

107. Cat

Throughout history, cats have been considered both lucky and unlucky. They were sacred to the ancient Egyptians, and it was a capital offense to kill one. Freya, the Norse goddess of marriage, rode in a carriage pulled by cats. Christians denounced Freya as a witch when they tried to eradicate Pagan practices. The cats that accompanied her were also denounced, so people started believing that cats were agents of Satan. Even today, the popular impression of a witch is an old lady accompanied by a black cat. The image of cats improved when soldiers returning home from the Crusades unintentionally brought black rats with them. This caused the Great Plague that killed millions of people. Suddenly, cats were needed again.

Because they are sensitive, aloof, and enjoy being outdoors at night, people have always thought cats have psychic abilities. A cat charm helps people develop their psychic potential and attract good luck. A multicolored cat charm is believed to be especially lucky.

In Japan, shop owners use a cat charm, known as a *maneki neko* to attract customers. This is a porcelain cat that sits with one paw raised in the air. It looks as if this cat is waving, but in actuality it is beckoning in wealth. You can see examples of maneki neko in many Asian restaurants and Asian-owned stores around the world.

108. Chestnuts

Chestnuts have been a symbol of good luck for thousands of years. This may be because they're pleasant to hold, but it's more likely to be because they're a winter food. In ancient Chinese astrology, the chestnut corresponded to autumn and the west.

See also BUCKEYE.

109. Coal

In the past, soldiers, sailors, thieves, and anyone else involved in potentially dangerous work carried a small piece of coal with them to attract good luck. The coal is especially lucky if it is given to you by a chimney sweep. You can keep it in your purse or pocket. If you happen to find a piece of coal, instead of carrying it you can spit on it and then toss it over your left shoulder to ensure good luck. Don't look back to see where it landed.

You can ensure good luck and prosperity for the family in the coming year by bringing in some coal on New Year's Day. This needs to be the first thing you do when you get up, and the coal must be brought in through the front door for the luck to work.

A charming theatrical tradition says you can toss a lump of coal from the stage up to the gallery to ensure the success of any new theater.

110. Coins

The concept of lucky coins goes back to the ancient Greeks, who tossed coins into wells to ensure they always had water. Even today, it's considered good luck to toss a coin into a fountain, river, or well. Many people carry a lucky penny around with them to attract good luck. The luckiest coin you can carry is one that was minted in the year of your birth. A coin that was minted in a leap year is said to be twice as lucky as a regular coin. The first coin that comes into your possession at the start of a new year is also said to be lucky. You should not spend this, but keep it as a lucky coin for the next twelve months.

Some people always carry a few coins with them in their pocket or purse because they believe it will attract more money to them.

It's a sign of a sudden increase in your fortunes if you happen to find three coins, all bearing the same date, in your pocket.

It's good luck to find a coin, and it's extremely good luck if the coin happens to be heads up.

It's good luck to keep a penny that was minted in a leap year in your kitchen. This is said to bring good luck to the entire household.

A bent coin makes an extremely effective good luck charm. However, you cannot bend the coin yourself. To be lucky, you need to find it already bent.

An ancient tradition says that if you have a silver coin in your pocket, you should turn it over and make a wish when seeing either the full moon or the new moon. This wish, so it is said, will be granted. If you happen to notice the moon is in its first quarter (when the crescent moon faces left) when you're out at night, turn over all the coins in your pocket, and you'll enjoy financial good luck for the next month. It's important that you do not remove the coins from your pocket when turning them over.

You can turn your lucky coin into a pendant, or keep it in your pocket or purse. Look after it, though, as your luck will decrease if you lose it.

If you find a coin anywhere you should always pick it up, no matter how small its value. This is because it's always good luck to find money, as long as you pick it up.

If you're putting on a new item of clothing for the first time and it has a pocket, place a coin inside. If you do this, you'll always enjoy good luck while wearing it.

111. Cornucopia

The cornucopia, or horn of plenty, is a horn overflowing with flowers, fruits, and grains. The concept dates back to Greek mythology. Zeus accidentally broke off the horn of the goat that was suckling him. When he gave it to his nurse, the horn began providing unlimited quantities of food and drink. Ever since, the cornucopia has been a symbol of abundance and good luck. If you wear a charm in the shape of a cornucopia, you'll always have enough of everything you need.

112. Crickets

Crickets have been considered lucky for thousands of years. Their chirping provided company as well as a warning of potential danger. At the first sign of anything untoward, crickets stop chirping. It's considered bad luck to kill a cricket. In ancient times, charms in the shape of a cricket were used to ward off the evil eye. In China, crickets were kept in cages, as they symbolized summer, bravery, happiness, and good luck. Today charms in the shape of crickets are used to attract happiness and good luck.

113. Daisies and Dandelions

Daisies and dandelions are traditional symbols of love and romance. There can't be many people who haven't plucked off the petals of a daisy one at a time while chanting, "S/he loves me, s/he loves me not." The final petal provides the answer. As children, we used to do this by blowing the cottony top of the dandelion, reciting the phrase with each blow. Another version of this was to make a wish, close your eyes, and then blow vigorously at the dandelion. If the entire top came off in a single blow, the wish would be granted.

Wearing a charm in the shape of a daisy or dandelion is believed to provide good luck and also attract the right partner to you.

114. Daruma Doll

The Daruma doll is the most popular good luck charm in Japan. Daruma was a sixth-century monk who meditated for so long that he lost the ability to use his arms and legs. Consequently, the Daruma doll is egg-shaped. When it's knocked over, it immediately becomes upright again, symbolizing perseverance, ultimate success, and good luck. When you buy a Daruma doll, both eyes are white. To activate the doll, you paint a pupil in one eye and make a wish. When the wish comes true you paint in the other eye, and then buy a slightly larger doll and start the process over again.

Daruma dolls can be found in gift shops and online. I was introduced to them while in Japan many years ago, and have used several Daruma dolls since then. I like the fact that they force you to think of a specific desire. You are reminded of this goal every time you see the doll, and it's a highly satisfying moment when the goal has been accomplished and you can paint in the second pupil.

115. Dog

Dogs have been considered our best friends for at least twenty thousand years. Dogs are friendly, loyal, obedient, loving, and forgiving. These qualities, as well as good luck, are said to be bestowed on people who wear a charm in the shape of a dog. Dog charms are often worn for protection.

116. Dolphin

Charms in the shape of dolphins have become extremely popular in recent years. It's no wonder why—they're friendly, intelligent, and playful mammals. In Greek and Etruscan mythology, dolphins always helped mankind. They saved people from drowning and carried souls to the Islands of the Blessed. The poet Arion is an example of someone saved from drowning. A statue of him riding a dolphin was erected at the Temple of Poseidon in Cape Sounion, Greece.

The dolphin is considered lucky because sailors in ancient times loved seeing them swimming around their ships, as it meant land was near. A dolphin charm provides protection and good luck.

117. Eggs

Eggs symbolize fertility, purity, spring, perfection, and the Immaculate Conception. Eggs feature frequently in creation myths around the world. It's considered good luck to give someone a white egg. It's even better to give a brown egg, as that provides both good luck and happiness.

An egg charm usually shows a baby chicken emerging from the egg. Sometimes, the egg is surrounded by grass and leaves.

118. Elephant

Elephants symbolize wisdom, strength, fidelity, prosperity, and longevity. Ganesh, the Hindu god of wisdom and luck, has the head of an elephant. Elephant charms became popular in Europe and the United States in the early part of the twentieth century. In charms, elephants are normally depicted with their trunks upraised, as these are believed to be luckier than elephants depicted in other positions.

119. Four-Leaf Clover

Four-leaf clovers have been considered lucky for thousands of years. The origins of the lucky four-leaf clover are unknown. An old legend tells how Eve took a four-leaf clover with her when she and Adam were expelled from the Garden of Eden. It was to remind her of the blissful life she had lost forever. An old nursery rhyme relates each of the four leaves to different aspects of life:

> One leaf is for fame,
> And one leaf is for wealth,
> And one is for a faithful lover,
> And one to bring you glorious health,
> Are all in the four-leaved clover.

It's a sign of good luck to find a four-leaf clover. You should dry it between two sheets of blotting paper, and then keep it in a cellophane envelope or small plastic bag. It will remain a potent lucky charm as long as you carry it with you.

120. Frog

Frogs were considered so important in ancient Egypt that they were embalmed after death. In the first century CE, Pliny the Elder (23–79) wrote that frog charms attracted friends and everlasting love. The Greeks associated frogs with Aphrodite, because of their noisy love-play. Consequently, they became a symbol of fertility. Frogs are a popular good luck charm in Japan, especially for travelers. This is because the Japanese word for frog is *kaeru*. The same word also means "to return home." Many Japanese people carry small frog charms close to their money, to ensure it won't be lost. In China, the frog symbolizes a happy home and family life.

In America, it's considered a sign of good luck if a frog happens to enter your home. You should also make a wish when you first see a frog in spring.

Frog charms have been popular for attracting luck for at least two thousand years.

121. Hand

The hand symbolizes power and strength. Charms in the shape of hands have always been considered lucky, as they allow you to receive whatever is rightfully yours. The palm of the hand provides protection by pushing away any negativity. Hand charms almost always depict the right hand, as this is considered the lucky hand, and it's also the hand of God. The left hand used to be associated with the devil and was considered unlucky.

Some charms show the hand with the first two fingers extended and the thumb, third, and fourth fingers closed. This is a sign of a blessing.

122. Heart

The ancient Egyptians believed the heart was the seat of the soul and intellect, and the body died when the soul left the heart. Many people believe that their hearts will be weighed at the day of judgment, and only people with perfect hearts will be allowed into the afterlife. Today, the heart is considered a token of pure love, and lovers frequently exchange heart-shaped charms to symbolize this perfect love. In addition to this, heart-shaped charms provide protection and good luck to the wearer.

123. Holly

Holly was a symbol of friendship in ancient Rome, and people would send it to each other as a gift. Holly gradually became associated with love and marriage. Consequently, it was a custom for single people to sometimes wear a holly charm to help them attract a suitable partner. Married people can also wear holly charms, as this ensures their relationship will be a happy one. Placing a holly charm under your pillow is said to help resolve marital problems.

The holly tree has always been considered lucky. The ancient Druids believed it had special powers as it remained evergreen throughout winter. It's considered unlucky to cut down a holly tree.

124. Horse

Charms in the shape of a horse are usually white or black. A white horse attracts good luck, while a black horse symbolizes mystery and sophistication. (However, though they seldom appear as charms, it's considered lucky to unexpectedly see a gray horse.) All horse charms represent strength and courage. In the East, the horse symbolizes happiness and a successful career. It's one of the twelve animals in the Chinese horoscope.

125. Horseshoe

Horseshoes are considered lucky for a number of reasons. Horses have always been considered lucky animals. Horseshoes are made from iron, which is also considered lucky. The U-shape of the horseshoe is considered a sign of protection.

Horseshoes should be hung over a doorway. It is better to hang it outdoors, as this enables it to bring luck to the house and everyone living in it. If the horseshoe is hung with the prongs facing upward, it symbolizes a container full of good luck. If the prongs face downward, this good luck will be distributed throughout the house.

You can buy a horseshoe to hang over a door, but it's considered luckier to either find it or be given one. If there are nails in it when you obtain it, you mustn't remove them, as each nail represents a full year of good luck. Use the horseshoe's own nails if possible. Always attach the horseshoe with an odd number of nails to maximize the good luck.

It's an extremely lucky omen to find a horseshoe. When this occurs you should pick it up and nail it over the entrance to your home. Alternatively, you could pick it up, and spit on it while making a wish. Once you've done that, you should throw it over your left shoulder. It's important that you don't look back to see where it landed. It's also important that you pick up a horseshoe when you find one, as you'll receive no good luck from it if you simply walk past.

126. Kachina Doll

Kachina are the protective ancestral spirits of the Native American Hopi tribe. They emerge from the earth at the start of the winter solstice and provide protection until the summer solstice begins. Kachina dolls represent these ancestral spirits. The dolls are painted in six colors that relate to the six cardinal directions: yellow for north, white for east, red for south, turquoise for west, black for sky, and gray for earth.

Kachina dolls are displayed in the home and are also used as childrens' toys. This is because the spirit represented by the doll is believed to bring good luck to the household if it becomes an integral part of the family.

127. Ladybird or Ladybug

Ladybug charms are often worn as brooches to attract prosperity and good luck. Seeing a ladybug is a sign of good luck, and it's even more fortunate if it lands on you. If it does, count the number of spots it has. This indicates the number of lucky months ahead of you. Allow the ladybug to fly away when it's ready. You'll lose all the good luck it has provided if you force it to leave by brushing it off. It has always been considered bad luck to kill a ladybug.

The ladybug or ladybird received its current name during the Middle Ages. At that time, it was dedicated to the Virgin Mary and was known as the "beetle of our lady." [3]

When I was a child, I used to place a ladybird on a finger and recite a nursery rhyme before blowing at it. Invariably, it would fly away. The origins of the nursery rhyme are not known, and it first appeared in printed form in 1744.

Ladybird, ladybird,
fly away home.
Your house is on fire
and your children all gone;
all except one
and that's little Ann
and she has crept under
the warming pan.

The most likely explanation of this old rhyme is the traditional burning of the hop vines after harvest. This was done to clear the fields, and many ladybugs were killed in the process.

128. Leaves

Leaves symbolize vibrant health and an abundance of energy. Because of this, charms showing a number of leaves are often worn to provide protection from colds and other minor ailments, especially in winter.

See also FOUR-LEAF CLOVER.

129. Leprechaun

Good luck charms depicting a tiny elf-like shoemaker wearing a red or green coat and wielding a hammer are especially popular in Ireland but can also be found on charm bracelets in many parts of the world. Leprechauns are tiny people who, according to legend, keep their treasure in pots hidden at the end of rainbows. Traditionally, the leprechauns will give their treasure to anyone who sees them, but this is extremely hard to do as leprechauns are wily, tricky people who love practical jokes.

Despite the many misfortunes the Irish have suffered over the years, they have always been associated with good luck, as the phrase "luck of the Irish" attests.

130. Lizard

Lizard charms are often worn as finger rings, though they are also found as brooches and pendants. They attract good luck and are also often worn to enhance the person's eyesight. This is because the emerald green color of many lizards symbolizes the gem, which is believed to improve vision.

It's considered good luck for a pregnant woman to see a lizard, as this indicates her unborn baby will live a long, happy, productive life.

131. Mandrake

The mandrake is the root of the mandragora plant. The turnip-like root is often forked, making the root look like a small person. Because of this, the mandrake has been used as an aphrodisiac for thousands of years. It is even mentioned in the Bible (Genesis 30:14, and Song of Solomon 7:13).[4] The mandrake was used as a charm in the Middle Ages to provide fertility, happiness, and abundance. Some people carried entire roots around their necks, but it was more usual for small figures to be carved from the roots and worn as charms.[5] If you'd like to experiment with mandrake roots, it's not necessary to carve your own figure nowadays. Metal and ceramic charms representing them can be found in gift stores and online.

132. Mistletoe

The charming tradition of kissing under the mistletoe began in Scandinavia. Enemies who wished to resolve their differences would meet under the mistletoe and exchange a kiss of peace.[6] It didn't take long for people to realize that any two people could kiss under the mistletoe, and so the happy tradition began. Not surprisingly, a mistletoe charm is worn to attract love and romance. It also ensures the relationship is a long one.

Mistletoe was revered by the ancient druids, and was considered especially sacred if found growing on an oak tree.

It's good luck to hang mistletoe in the busiest part of your home over the Christmas period. Every time someone is kissed under the mistletoe, the happiness, wealth, and luck of the family is increased. This good luck works only when the mistletoe is hung in your home. However, it's good luck for the individual to be kissed under mistletoe anywhere.

133. Nail

It's a sign of good luck to find a nail when you're out and about. The rustier the nail is, the better, as rust increases the luck. To activate this luck, take the nail home with you.

If you wish, you can carry the nail around with you as a protective amulet. Alternatively, you can hammer the nail into the frame of your back door to provide protection for your home. The nail needs to be hammered in with four strokes of the hammer. With the first stroke, say out loud: "Once for luck." Say, "Once for health" on the second stroke, "Once for love" on the third, and "Once for money" on the fourth.

134. Owl

The large, slow-blinking eyes that owls possess have always made people think they are wise. Consequently, owls symbolize wisdom, knowledge, and common sense. Owl charms are usually worn to attract these qualities, though some people keep them close to their wallets and purses, as they are also believed to attract prosperity.

If you're fortunate enough to find an owl's feather, keep it as a lucky charm that will protect you from envy and other forms of negativity.

135. Parik-Til

A *parik-til*, or blessing holder, is similar to Native American medicine bags. It is custom for Romani people to keep them as lucky charms, and they can be made for any purpose. All you need is a small drawstring bag.

You can put anything inside it you would like as long as the items relate to your goal in some sort of way. If you intend using it to attract good luck, you might place an acorn, a stone you found, a small piece of gold, a note from you requesting good luck, a small lucky charm of a horseshoe, and a coin inside a green drawstring bag. The gold could be a gold coin, but it may be a mere fragment from a broken piece of jewelry. You might like to add a few drops of a favorite perfume to scent the bag.

Place the bag and the objects in direct sunlight for at least two hours. Place everything inside the bag, add perfume if desired, and carry the parik-til with you as a lucky charm. At least once a day, give it some attention—tell it of your need for more good luck in your life. To ensure continued good luck, continue doing this, even after you've attained whatever it was you were seeking.

136. Pearl

Pearls have been valued for thousands of years. In ancient Rome, people below a certain rank were not allowed to wear them.[7] In India, the pearl is one of the nine stones in the Navratna, the most revered of all Indian charms. Pearls provide respect, kindness, sympathy, and love. A single pearl is believed to revitalize the body and provide peace of mind. People who wear pearls are believed to enjoy happy, harmonious lives.

There are many superstitions about pearls, mainly based on the idea that a pearl is symbolically the tear of an oyster. Consequently, if you're given a pearl or pearls, you should pay a small sum for them to avoid shedding tears. Even as little as a penny is sufficient. If you don't, the superstition says you will shed many tears. Some brides refuse to wear pearls on their wedding day, as they believe they cause them to start their married lives with sorrow. However, it is good luck to give a pearl to a baby, as it ensures he or she will enjoy a long life.

137. Pentacle

The pentacle is a five-pointed star enclosed within a circle. It is usually worn with a single point facing upward, as this traditionally invokes good, positive energy. It's considered a symbol of black magic or evil if two points face upward. The pentacle has a great deal of symbolism attached to it. The five points indicate the five senses. They can also indicate a person, with the points representing a head, two arms, and two legs. Leonardo da Vinci's famous *Vitruvian Man* depicts the proportions of a man, and is an example of this. It consists of a circle, enclosing a naked man with his arms and legs outstretched. As the circle is a feminine symbol of protection, this creates a picture of male and female harmony. Because of this, pentacle charms often consist of a circle with the pentacle inside.

The pentacle dates back four thousand years to ancient Mesopotamia and was possibly created to represent the movements of the planet Venus. It's possible that it was the figure on the Seal of Solomon, though some experts believe that may have been a hexagram. The ancient Pythagoreans adopted it as a symbol of good health and harmony. They felt it symbolized the marriage of heaven and earth, as it combined the number two (earth and female) with three (heaven and male). Early Christians associated the pentacle with the five wounds of Christ.

A pentacle charm attracts friendship, harmony, good luck, and a successful marriage. It is considered one of the most powerful of all good luck charms.

138. Phoenix

The phoenix is a symbol of rebirth. According to ancient Greek legend, the mythical phoenix lives for hundreds of years before making a nest of spices. The bird then sets fire to the nest by flapping its wings. The bird turns to ashes, and then returns to life again.

The phoenix is a useful charm for people who are seeking renewal or a new start. Many years ago, I knew a man who had suffered a business reversal. When he started again, he called his business Phoenix Construction. As well as having a phoenix on his letterhead and business cards, he also wore a small phoenix brooch on the jacket of his suit. He believed implicitly that the phoenix helped him make a success of his second business.

139. Pig

Miniature silver pigs are frequently found on charm bracelets. This is because possession of a pig ensured the family's success and survival in previous centuries. It also explains why money boxes are often piggy banks. The shape is believed to protect the money inside it and also attract more.

The German word for pig is *schwein*, and *schwein haben* means "be lucky." In Chinese culture, pigs are believed to be brave, honest, and diligent.

Because of the pig's association with prosperity, a pig charm attracts wealth as well as good luck.

140. Rabbit's Foot

Rabbits' feet, especially the left hind foot, are believed to be protective, as well as lucky. The hind legs of a rabbit touch the ground before the front feet. This was considered so extraordinary that the back feet were credited with magical powers. In addition to this, rabbits are extremely fertile, and in past centuries farmers wanted large families to help cultivate the fields. Finally, rabbits are born with their eyes open, and this gives them power over the evil eye. No wonder rabbits' feet were considered a sign of good luck.

When I was a child, we always said "white rabbits" on the first of every month, as this was supposed to provide a whole month of good luck. These words had to be said before saying anything else. Some people repeat these words three times, and others simply say "rabbits."

Rabbit's foot charms are still extremely popular today.

141. Rose

Roses have been considered symbols of perfection for thousands of years. White roses signify purity, innocence, and virginity, while red roses relate to love and passion. Roman emperors wore wreaths made of roses as crowns, and rose petals were scattered on graves during the festival of Rosaria. They also wore rose garlands at their Bacchanalian revels, as they believed the garlands would control drunkenness and loose talk. Hundreds of years later, roses were hung or painted above council tables to show that everything spoken there was private. This is where the expression *sub rosa* came from. Christians relate the red rose with its thorns to the sufferings of Christ and his love for all mankind.

A red rose charm symbolizes faithfulness and protects the relationship. A white rose charm symbolizes purity in thought, word, and deed.

142. St. Christopher Medal

The figure of St. Christopher is one of the most popular good luck charms of all. St. Christopher is the patron saint of travelers, and millions of people carry a St. Christopher medal with them when they are away from home. I know a number of people who keep one in their car. This medal provides protection and good luck.

St. Christopher was a third-century Christian martyr. An old legend says that he lived beside a river and helped travelers make the crossing. One day, he carried a child over the river. The child became increasingly heavy, and Christopher barely made it to the other side. When he mentioned this to the child, the boy told him that he had just borne all the world and its sins on his shoulders. He had crossed the river of Death, and the child was Jesus Christ. The name Christopher comes from the

Latin word *christophorus*, which means "one who carries Christ." The St. Christopher medal shows the saint carrying the child.

143. Scarab

The ancient Egyptians watched the dung beetle using its rear legs to roll balls of dung to its underground home for food. Because it can't see where it's going, the beetle often takes a circuitous route to its home. The action reminded the Egyptians of the sun's daily journey across the sky. The beetle eggs laid inside the ball of dung eventually hatch, symbolizing creation. Because of all this, it's not surprising that the scarab is one of the best-known Egyptian charms. In fact, hundreds of thousands of them were made over a period of two thousand years.[8]

A scarab charm symbolizes birth, regeneration, good health, and virility.

144. Shell

Shells have been used as lucky charms for thousands of years. Because you can hear a sound like waves pounding on a beach when you place a conch shell to your ear, people thought this created a connection between people on land and those at sea. Consequently, shells became lucky charms that ensured sailors and fishermen would return home safely.

145. Ship

The ancient Egyptians believed a ship transported the sun on its nightly journey through the underworld. Early Christians used charms in the shape of ships to provide protection while they were crossing over water. They also believed that ship charms symbolically carried believers across the sea of life to the Promised Land. This belief gradually expanded to protect the wearer from the sins of the flesh, to ensure that he or she was saved.

A ship charm relates to security, no matter what is going on in the wearer's life.

146. Snake

The snake is a symbol of regeneration as it sheds its skin and appears to become a new snake. In Greek and Roman times, the snake symbolized vitality and good health. This symbology can still be seen today in the Rod of Asclepius, the emblem of medicine, which shows a rod entwined by a serpent or snake. Early Christians disliked snakes, as one offered Eve the forbidden fruit in the Garden of Eden.

A snake charm provides protection against enemies and anyone who may be conspiring against you. It also provides intelligence, insight, and longevity.

147. Spider

It's considered fortunate to see a spider. In England, people used to believe that money would be coming their way if a spider landed on their clothing. It is considered bad luck to kill a spider.

A spider charm is said to provide good luck and protection from unexpected problems. It can help decision making, especially in matters involving money.

An old tradition says you'll have good luck forever if you find your initials inside a spider's web.

148. Star

An ancient belief says that we all have a guiding star, one that appeared in the sky when we were born, and which will disappear when we die. Napoleon and Adolf Hitler are just two people who believed they had a "star of destiny."

Someone who was "born under a lucky star" experiences constant good luck as he or she progresses through life.

Wearing a charm in the shape of a star helps you attract some of the good luck that people who were born under a lucky star are supposed to experience all the time.

149. Tortoise and Turtle

Tortoise-shaped amulets dating back to the Neolithic period have been found in Egypt. This means they date back nine thousand years. This makes them one of the oldest of all magical objects.[9]

When worn as a charm, the tortoise gives patience, stability, longevity, and good fortune.

150. Lucky Flowers of the Zodiac

Certain flowers are associated with each sign of the zodiac. You can display, and in some cases wear, the flowers that relate to your sign to attract good luck. Many of them can also be bought as brooches or charms. Another possibility is to carry a small picture of your chosen flower in your wallet or purse. Whenever you see it, it will remind you how lucky you are.

+ Aries: Anemone, daffodil, hawthorn, honeysuckle, and nasturtium.

+ Taurus: Cherry, forget-me-not (shared with Scorpio), and red rose.

+ Gemini: Hazel, iris, lavender (shared with Virgo), and London pride.

+ Cancer: Clover, daisy, honesty (moonwort), and white poppy.

+ Leo: Marigold, peony, and sunflower.

+ Virgo: Lavender (shared with Gemini), and lily-of-the-valley.

+ Libra: Love-in-a-mist, violet, and white rose.

+ Scorpio: Chrysanthemum, forget-me-not (shared with Taurus), and orchid.

- Sagittarius: Clove carnation (shared with Pisces), ivy (shared with Capricorn), and lilac.

- Capricorn: Ivy (shared with Sagittarius), jasmine, Christmas rose, and snowdrop (shared with Aquarius).

- Aquarius: Amaranth, mimosa, spring crocus, and snowdrop (shared with Capricorn).

- Pisces: Clove carnation (shared with Sagittarius), pink gardenia, goat's beard, love-in-a-mist, and sweet violet.

— Part Three —

Luck by Category

Most people want to enjoy a long-lasting, compatible relationship with a loving partner. They also want a happy home life and the chance to make the most of the time at their disposal. Luck comes into all of these, and in this section we'll discuss the various methods people have used to encourage good luck in these areas of their lives.

Six

....

Love and Marriage

Introduction

My wife and I have been happily married for more than forty years. Some of our friends have been married for many years, too. We also have friends who have been married a number of times, and friends who are single and searching for the right partner. It's not surprising that there are probably more suggestions on how to increase your luck in the area of love and marriage than in any other aspect of life.

My wife and I know a middle-aged man who would love to meet a suitable woman and get married. However, he does absolutely nothing to help himself. He works at home, and leaves his house only to buy groceries and other supplies. At one time he placed advertisements on dating sites, but he didn't follow up on any of the leads he obtained. Unless he makes an effort, his chances of meeting women are almost zero. Luck often involves being in the right place at the right time. He's unlikely to meet anyone in his home. Consequently, his luck would increase enormously if he made an effort to visit more places. If he did that, sooner or later he'd start meeting people, and if he met enough of them, in time he'd probably find a partner. Here are a number of methods that people have used to become luckier in the areas of love and marriage. If you're seeking more luck in this area, remain positive, keep telling yourself that the right person is waiting for you to find him or her, and experiment with the suggestions in this chapter.

151. Kiss as Many People as Possible

In his book, *On Love*, Dr. Bubba Nicholson says that kissing is a highly effective way to taste and smell semiochemicals on people's skin. Semiochemicals enable people to subconsciously assess their degree of compatibility with other people. It follows that if you want to be lucky in love, you need to kiss as many people as possible until you find the right person for you.

152. Be Lovable

If you want to be loved, you need to be loving and lovable. This should continue long after the courtship and marriage. If you continue doing whatever it was that made you attractive in the first place, your relationship will continue to strengthen and grow.

153. Love Letters

Love letters are lucky for both the writer and recipient. However, as strong emotions are generated by writing and reading a love letter, numerous superstitions offer advice on when and how to write a suitable letter.

The best day to write a love letter is supposed to be Friday. This is because Friday is dedicated to Venus, the goddess of love. The word "Friday" comes from the Old English word *frigedaeg*, which means "Frige's (Freya's) day." Freya was the wife of the Norse god Odin. However, the word for "Friday" in most European languages comes from the Latin *dies Veneris*, which means "Venus's day." Consequently, Freya became connected to Venus, and Friday is considered Venus's day.

Love letters should not be typed or written in pencil. They should be written with a pen.

It's a good omen if your hand trembles while writing a love letter. This means that the recipient reciprocates your love.

Once written, the letter should not be posted on a Sunday, or for some unknown reason, on February 29, September 1, or December 25.

If you receive a love letter, you should examine the envelope carefully. If the flap has come open in the post, or if the stamp is of an incorrect value, it's a sign that there are problems in the relationship.

It's bad luck to propose by letter. You can exchange as many love letters as you wish, but save the proposal until you are together in person.

154. The Law of Attraction

The law of attraction says that whatever you ask for, the universe will provide. Consequently, if you're looking for a partner, you need to think carefully about all the desirable qualities you're looking for and send this thought out to the universe.

You do this by focusing on the qualities you desire as often as you can. Lying in bed before drifting off to sleep is a good time to do this. However, you should also do this at odd times during the day. You can think about your desire for a suitable partner while waiting in line, waiting for traffic lights to change, or traveling. We all get a certain amount of dead time during the day.

In the past, people tried a number of different methods to find a husband or wife. One common one was to carefully peel an apple, making sure to cut the skin into one long piece. Once that's been accomplished, you had to turn around three times and throw the skin over your shoulder. You could then examine the shape it created, as it should reveal the first letter of your future lover's name. You can do this whenever you wish, but the best day of the year for this experiment is October 28, which is the feast day of St. Simon and St. Jude.

Once you've found a potential partner, you can perform the traditional children's game of plucking the petals off a daisy while reciting, "S/he loves me, s/he loves me not."

155. Red Roses

As the rose is considered the flower of love, it's an extremely lucky sign for a young woman to dream of a rose. It's even luckier if she dreams of a red rose.

Women in England used to pick a red rose on Midsummer's Eve and wrap it carefully in white paper. They would then hide it in a safe place until Christmas Day. If the rose still appeared fresh, the woman would wear it to church on Christmas morning. Her future husband would see it, and either compliment her on the rose or remove it. If the rose had died, the woman would remain single for another year.

Roses could also be used to determine the depth of someone's love. The person enquiring about the degree of love had to snap the stem of a rose. The louder the noise, the more passionate and devoted the person would be.

In Victorian times, when couples were nearly constantly chaperoned, flowers were used to convey secret messages. In this system, red roses symbolized passion and white roses pure, chaste love.

Cupid is said to have been stung by a bee while admiring a beautiful rose bush. He became so angry that he shot an arrow at the bush, and the bush bled, causing all the flowers to turn red. Another story involving Cupid says that he accidentally spilled red wine over a rose bush, turning the roses red.

156. Love at First Sight

The ancient Greeks believed that man and woman were originally one. The gods cut them into two to weaken them, as they thought humankind was planning to overthrow them. This, they believed, was the reason why people could fall in love at first sight. They were simply recognizing the other half of their original selves.

Geoffrey Chaucer (c. 1343–1400) wrote: "She lovede right from the firste sighte" (*Troilus and Criseyde*, 1375); Christopher Marlowe (1564–1593), the Elizabethan playwright, wrote: "Whoever loved, that loved not at first sight!" (*Hero and Leander*, 1598).

A tiny purple flower called love-in-idleness is associated with love at first sight, because an old legend says that Cupid's arrow pierced one of these flowers. William Shakespeare (1564–1616) the English dramatist, made fun of the concept of love at first sight by suggesting that placing a small tincture of liquid from one of these flowers on the eyelids of a sleeping person "will make a man or woman wildly dote upon the next live creature that it sees" (*A Midsummer's Night's Dream*, act II, scene i). In Shakespeare's tragedy, *Romeo and Juliet*, Romeo falls in love at first sight.

Love at first sight is not impossible, as attractiveness can be determined in a fraction of a second, and a few minutes conversation can determine the compatibility or otherwise of the two people concerned.

If you want to be lucky enough to fall in love at first sight, be extremely vigilant on the seventh day after the full moon. According to tradition, this is the most likely day for two people to fall in love at first sight.

157. Mirror, Mirror, on the Wall

There are many superstitions involving mirrors. The best-known one is that if you break a mirror, you'll experience seven years of bad luck. Fortunately, there are also positive superstitions involving mirrors, including two ways in which a young woman can see an image of her future lover. A tradition from the Deep South of the United States says a woman can hold a mirror over a well and see in it a picture of her future husband.

In the United Kingdom, it's said that if a woman places a mirror under her pillow, she'll be able to see her future husband in her dreams.

You can also stand in front of a mirror and brush your hair three times before going to bed. If you do this, you may experience dreams involving you and your future lover.

158. Flower Power

Flowers play a major role in the folklore of love and marriage. You could ensure the continued faithfulness and love of the person you desired by planting marigold seeds in earth that your desired person had walked on. The plants need to be well tended, as the love will grow as long as the plants continue to thrive.

It's a sign of love in the near future if you dream of a red rose.

If you want to attract a lover, put fresh daisies under your pillow every night before going to bed. You are likely to have vivid dreams involving your future lover. Continue doing this until you meet the right person.

You can also see your future lover in your dreams if you sprinkle a sprig of rosemary and a sprig of thyme with water three times, and then place one in each of your shoes. Place the shoes at the foot of your bed immediately before going to sleep.

159. Lucky Days for Proposals

Traditionally, the man always proposed to the woman, except in a leap year when it was acceptable for a woman to propose to a man. Nowadays, it doesn't matter much who does the proposing, but whoever it is should pay some attention to the day of the week on which the proposal is to be made.

The couple will lead happy and eventful lives if the proposal is made on a Monday. They will enjoy harmonious lives together if the proposal is made on a Tuesday. They will never argue if the proposal is made on a Wednesday. They will both achieve their major goals if the proposal is made on a Thursday. They will need to work hard to achieve success if the proposal is made on a Friday. They will enjoy a highly compatible, harmonious life together if the proposal is made on a Saturday. Traditionally, a proposal should never be made on a Sunday, as that is the Lord's day.

160. The Wedding Day

Once the right partner has been found, it's traditional to get married. Certain days are considered lucky, and it makes good sense to select one of them. Here are some of the things you need to consider.

The ancient Romans honored their dead in May, and during this month everyone wore mourning clothes. Even now, two thousand years later, May is not considered a good month to get married in. The old saying "marry in May, and you'll rue the day" still seems to apply. Conversely, June is considered an extremely lucky month to get married in. This is because in Roman mythology Juno and Jupiter were married in June. June was Juno's month, and the ancient Romans liked to have their weddings in that month to ensure her blessing. Two thousand years later, June is still an extremely popular month to get married in.

You shouldn't get married during Lent (the six weeks before Easter), or on Childermas (December 28), Maundy Thursday (the Thursday before Easter), St. Swithin's Day (July 15), or St. Thomas's Day (December 21).

You also need to be careful which day of the week to get married on. An old nursery rhyme goes:

Monday for wealth,
Tuesday for health,
Wednesday, the best day of all.
Thursday for losses,
Friday for crosses,
Saturday no luck at all.

Saturday was disliked, as superstitious people believed one of the partners would die early. However, Saturday is now the most popular day for weddings, as most people have the weekend off.

Of course, even following all of this, you still need to be lucky with the weather. Getting married on a wet, rainy day portends a difficult marriage, compared to the old saying: "Blessed is the bride that the sun shines on."

161. The Engagement Ring

The engagement ring is the first visible sign that a couple is going to get married. Certain stones in the engagement ring are supposed to be luckier than others. The luckiest stones are diamonds, emeralds, rubies, and sapphires. Opal is an unlucky stone for most people, but is lucky for women born in October. As pearls symbolize tears, they're considered unlucky in an engagement ring.

Friends of the bride-to-be can place the engagement ring on the tip of one of their fingers and make a wish, which will always be granted.

162. The Wedding Dress

To increase the amount of good luck in a marriage, the bride needs to wear "something old, something new, something borrowed, something blue."

The "something old" is often the wedding veil, which was originally worn to protect the bride from the dreaded evil eye. The veil is often a family heirloom. The veil may also be "something borrowed." In this case, it's important that the veil belongs to someone who is, or was, happily married. The veil should not be worn before the ceremony, and it's bad luck for the bride to see herself in a mirror while wearing it. Sometimes the "something old" is a piece of family jewelry, or some other item that has been in the family for a long time.

The "something new" is usually the wedding gown. The "something borrowed" often comes from a happily married woman who is a friend of the family. "Something blue" relates to fidelity, love, and purity. Often a blue garter is worn to satisfy this requirement. It's common for a bride to place a coin in her shoe, as this ensures good fortune in the marriage.

Sometimes the final stitch in the wedding dress is not completed until immediately before the bride leaves for her wedding. This provides her with additional good luck.

It's extremely good luck for the bride if she gets married in the same wedding dress as her mother.

Silk is arguably the best material for the wedding dress. This is because it increases the bride's luck.

163. The Wedding Ring

The charming custom of exchanging wedding rings dates back at least two thousand years. Tertullian (c. 160–c. 225), an early Christian writer, mentions a golden ring that was sent to the bride as a formal promise that the marriage would take place. William Shakespeare referred to the exchange of rings in *Twelfth Night* (1602):

A contract of eternal bond of love,
Confirm'd by mutual joinder of your hands,
Attested by the holy close of lips,
Strengthen'd by interchangement of your rings. (act V, scene i)

The Puritans tried to abolish the wedding ring, saying it was a heathen superstition. However, the custom continued, and it would be hard to imagine a wedding today in which the bride did not receive a wedding ring. In fact, nowadays, the groom almost always receives a wedding ring, too.

164. The Bridesmaids

The custom of bridesmaids dates back to times when people opposed to the marriage would try to carry the bride away. The bridesmaids had to protect the bride and make sure this didn't happen.

It can be lucky to be a bridesmaid, as it's expected that she'll receive a proposal of marriage herself within twelve months. However, it's bad luck to be a bridesmaid three times, as this means you'll become an old maid. Fortunately, there is a remedy. You need to become a bridesmaid four more times, making a total of seven, and all the bad luck will disappear.

It's very lucky for the bride to have a matron of honor. This is because the presence of a happily married woman in the bridal party symbolizes the wedded bliss that the bride can expect.

165. Rice and Confetti

The custom of throwing confetti over the bride and groom as they left the church is derived from an ancient practice of scattering corn on the head of the bride. Corn was a symbol of abundance, and it ensured the young couple would lead happy, and hopefully prosperous, lives with plenty of children. Wheat was frequently used instead of corn. Rice gradually replaced corn and wheat, and was in turn superseded by confetti.

166. The Wedding Cake

The wedding cake is an essential part of the wedding celebration, as it brings good luck to everyone who eats it. Traditionally, absent friends are sent a slice of the cake to ensure they can share in the good luck.

The cake should be rich and tasty, as this symbolizes abundance in the marriage.

The bride always cuts the first piece of cake, and makes a silent wish. If someone else cuts the first slice, the bride risks not having any children. This is because the wedding cake also symbolizes numerous offspring. Usually, the groom helps his bride cut the first slice by placing his hand over hers. This enables him to share in his bride's good fortune.

Sometimes the bride keeps a tier of her wedding cake to be used as a christening cake. This ensures the couple will produce children.

In England, small pieces of cake used to be passed through the bride's wedding ring nine times and given to the bridesmaids. Later, they would be placed under their pillows to enable them to dream of their future lovers.

167. Get Me to the Chapel on Time

If the bride's family has a cat, the bride needs to feed it, as this will ensure a long and happy marriage. (Interestingly, it's also a sign of good luck if the cat sneezes on the day before the wedding.)

On her way to the church, the bride-to-be has to leave her home by the front door, and step across the threshold with her right foot first. In the United Kingdom, it's good luck if the bride sees a black cat, a gray horse, an elephant, a rainbow, or a chimney sweep on her way to the church. Nowadays, as most people live in cities, it's unlikely that she'll see a gray horse or an elephant. However, it's possible to hire a chimney sweep who will happen to be in the right place at the right time, and offer good wishes to the bride.

Once she reached the church, the bride had to enter it again with her right foot first. She should not enter the church using a door that faces north.

168. The Bride's Bouquet

The bridal bouquet symbolizes fertility and the hope that the married couple will soon be blessed with a family. The ribbons tied around the bouquet also provide good luck.

The custom of the bride tossing her bouquet is an American tradition that began in the early years of the twentieth century and spread throughout the world. It supposedly began as a way in which the bride could misdirect the guests and, amid the confusion, leave the ceremony. Anything worn by the bride is considered lucky. Consequently, the lady who catches the bridal bouquet receives good luck, and is supposed to be the next person to get married.

169. Crossing the Threshold

It's traditional for the bridegroom to carry his new bride over the threshold. This is done to preserve the luck of the bride and groom in their new home. The origins of this tradition are unknown. However, there are two stories that are intended to explain it. One says it dates back to prehistoric times when men carried women off against their will to be their wives. By carrying her over the threshold, the groom symbolically carries his wife off to her new life. Another story says that it goes back to Roman times, and was a sign that the bride was giving up her virginity reluctantly. Either way, it's a pleasant tradition that brings luck to the happy couple.

170. Honeymoon

The honeymoon is the couple's first vacation together after the wedding. Samuel Johnson (1709–1784) described the honeymoon as "the first month after marriage, when there is nothing but tenderness and pleasure." No one knows where the term "honeymoon" originated, but it's possible it began in Babylon where newly married couples would drink alcohol made from honey for the first month of their marriage. The first literary reference to the word dates back to 1552 when it appeared in Richard Huloet's English-Latin dictionary, *Abecedarium Anglico-Latinum*. He made an ironic observation, saying that love, like the moon, inevitably waned.

Seven

....

Luck in the Home

Introduction

Your home is much more than a mere house. In many ways, your home is part of you, as it reflects your likes, dislikes, tastes, and personality. After the stresses and strains of everyday life, your home is a safe, nurturing, caring place to return to.

Many years ago, I helped a friend clear out his mother's home after she died. It was an amazing experience, as she'd never thrown anything away. There were huge piles of old newspapers, magazines, and junk mail everywhere, and we had to make our way down her hallway sideways, as there were stacks of papers from floor to ceiling on both sides. The rest of the house was also crammed with everything she'd accumulated over sixty years.

"Did no one ever suggest she clear out some of this stuff?" I asked.

My friend sighed. "Everyone did, all the time," he said. "She took no notice. She kept everything just in case she might find a use for it later."

I've thought of her house often over the years. I've seen many houses that were cluttered with too much stuff, but have never seen one as bad as hers.

All of us accumulate stuff all the time, but fortunately most people manage to keep it under some sort of control. I find it hard to part with books, but happily toss out anything else for which I don't have an immediate use.

In this chapter we'll start by looking at clutter and then examine a variety of other ways to help you attract luck to your home. If you are seeking luck in this area, don't try to implement everything all at once. Try one or two things at a time and observe what happens. If necessary, try something else and continue doing it until you experience the results you desire.

171. Clutter

Clutter is anything you no longer need, use, or love. Almost everyone has a favorite item they no longer use but find hard to toss out. This is because we develop an emotional attachment to things and convince ourselves that we will need whatever it happens to be one day.

We also gradually gain clutter in the form of unwanted gifts and objects we've been given over the years. It's hard to get rid of these, as they remind us of the person who gave them to us.

Other forms of clutter include items of clothing we've never worn and never will, and items left behind by family members who have moved away or into a home of their own.

Clutter belongs to the past. As long as you hang on to stuff you no longer need, you're holding yourself back. Decluttering your home sets you free and enables you to move forward again.

172. Feng Shui

Feng shui is the Chinese art of living in harmony with the earth. One of the key concepts of feng shui is ch'i, which can be described as energy or the universal life force.[1] Ch'i enters the home through the front door and should be able to move freely throughout the entire house. Anything that disrupts or blocks the flow of ch'i affects the good fortune and luck of the people living in the house. Clutter is a major factor in blocking good, positive ch'i energy. Once the clutter is brought under control, the people in the house will experience a sense of freedom, liberation, and greater energy. They'll also feel more confident, and find they're experiencing more good luck than ever before.

173. Activating the Ch'i

The ch'i should flow effortlessly through the house, entering through the front door and exiting out the back door and windows. Sometimes ch'i gets blocked. If the environment in the family is tense or someone is constantly argumentative or violent, the ch'i becomes stagnant and you can almost feel the tension in the house. Someone told me it reminded her of a black cloud that oppresses and limits everyone living in the house.

Emotional negativity can be eliminated by spraying water through a mister in every room. The misted water creates negative ions that allow the ch'i to flow freely again. Alternatively, you can use essential oils such as lavender, chamomile, or ylang ylang. These can be added to water and sprayed in each room, or you may choose to use an electrical diffuser that heats the oils.

A simple yet highly effective way to activate ch'i is to clap your hands vigorously in the room or rooms that need clearing. Make sure to clap in every part of the room, and visualize the energy moving as a result. Once you've finished clapping, wash your hands thoroughly in running water to eliminate any negative energy.

If someone has been ill for an extended period, you should first air out the room, and then activate the ch'i by misting with an essential oil such as lemon, eucalyptus, or rosemary.

You should thoroughly clean and air the room if someone has died in it. Once you've done that, use essential oils to encourage beneficial ch'i into the room again.

174. Smudging

It's a good idea to use a smudge stick or essential oils to activate your new home. This eliminates any negative energies left behind by the previous occupants.

You can make your own smudge sticks, but it isn't necessary, as they're readily available online, or from many New Age and natural health stores. They are made from a variety of different herbs, including cedar, rosemary, and sage. Try to buy one that contains sweetgrass, an herb that is particular good for eliminating negativity.

Start by changing into old clothes. Then light your smudge stick. Once it is burning well, extinguish the flames, and allow the herbs to smoulder. Smudge yourself before smudging your home. You do this by drawing the smudge stick from the top of your head down to your feet on one side, and repeating this on the other side. Once you've done this, you can smudge your house.

Although the flames have been extinguished, the smudge stick is still extremely hot. Consequently, you should hold a fireproof container under it as you walk through the house. Alternatively, you might ask someone else to hold the container so you can focus on the smudging.

Smudge each room in turn. Enter the house through the front door and start with the first room on the right. Waft the smoke into every corner of the room. Once you've finished a room, close the door as you leave. Work your way through the house until every room has been smudged.

Extinguish the smudge stick under running water. Repeat this every day until you feel a change in the energy of the house. Usually you'll begin to sense it after the second or third smudging session.

Wait for approximately half an hour before opening all the doors and windows. The smoke is extremely pungent, and you want to eliminate it once it's completed its task.

Once all the smoke has gone, you'll notice a subtle difference in your home. The energy will feel brighter, happier, and more energetic. The ch'i will be flowing freely, and good luck will come your way as a result.

175. Approach

To attract as much luck as possible, the pathway to your home should be clearly defined, and ideally be slightly curved. Any vegetation should be well tended and look healthy.

176. The Front Door

The entrance to your home is extremely important, as you want to encourage as much ch'i as possible into your home environment. Because of this, the front door should be well lit and appear welcoming. Any guests should be able to find your front door without any difficulty.

Items that are seldom used should not be kept in this area. Consequently, if there are several pairs of shoes stored either immediately inside or outside your front door, you should remove all of them except for those you wear regularly.

A friend of mine returned home from an overseas trip a few years ago. After unpacking his suitcase, he left it by the front door while deciding where to store it. Three years later, it was still there, and he was complaining that he never seemed to have enough money to take another trip. I suggested that he find a permanent home for his suitcase.

Anything that impedes the entrance of ch'i makes life more difficult for the people living in the home. Once you eliminate clutter from this area, more ch'i will come into your home and you'll receive more good luck in your everyday life.

177. The Back Door

The back door is where the ch'i leaves your home. Once the ch'i has spread throughout your home, you want it to be able to leave freely. It can't do that if this area is full of unused items. When I was in Singapore, a feng shui master told me that houses become constipated if the back door is impeded in any way.

178. Hallways

Hallways should be kept as clear as possible to allow ch'i to reach every part of the house. If the hallways are crowded with stuff, the ch'i will be impeded, and you'll feel limited and restricted in all areas of your life. Once the hallways have been cleared and are easy to walk through, the feelings of limitation will disappear and your good luck will return.

179. The Kitchen

The kitchen has always been considered the heart of the home. In days gone by, the family would gather around the kitchen fire for warmth and companionship. This no longer applies, but the kitchen should still be a warm and nurturing room for everyone living in the house. If you have too many unused items taking up space on the shelves of your kitchen, you'll feel powerless and hemmed in. Get rid of, or store, everything that is not being used on a regular basis, and you'll feel in control again.

I remember visiting a home that had several items on the kitchen counter that no longer worked. The owner was horrified when I suggested she get rid of them and replace them with objects that worked. She took my advice, though, and in a short space of time several positive things happened in her life. These included a visit from a long-lost son and a job offer.

The main entrance to the kitchen should be visible to whomever is doing the cooking, so they will not be surprised by someone walking into the kitchen unexpectedly.

Fridges and freezers should contain an abundance of food, as this relates to the family's prosperity. However, the food inside should be eaten on a regular basis, and replaced.

180. The Dining Room

The dining room should be a pleasant, relaxing room that makes people conducive to pleasant conversation. Ideally, the room should be self-contained. If it forms part of another room, it should have a clearly defined space of its own.

The dining room table should be the main focus of the room. Feng shui dictates that the best shapes are round, oval, and octagonal. Where someone sits at the table determines his or her ranking in the family. The power position, or the most important seat, should face the main entrance to the room.

The dining room should contain a few wall hangings or decorations that reflect the family's tastes and interests.

181. The Living Room

The living room should appear welcoming, relaxing, and comfortable. Because it's a room people relax in, it's common for items to be brought into this room and left there, rather than being returned to where they came from. Consequently, it's easy for this room to become cluttered. Too much clutter in this room will make you feel restless, anxious, and unable to relax.

Once you've decluttered your living room, you'll feel more relaxed in your own home and will start to experience good luck in your life again.

182. The Bathroom

Even the bathroom can become cluttered. If all the available surfaces are taken up with various items, you'll feel anxious and ill at ease. Removing old toothbrushes, cosmetics, and medications that are no longer being used (and anything else that is not required) will immediately make you feel more comfortable and relaxed. It will also increase your luck.

The bath and toilet should be inconspicuous. If possible, the toilet should be screened to provide privacy.

183. The Bedroom

The bedroom is a sanctuary, a place to relax, read, make love, sleep, and dream. Clutter in the bedroom affects all of these activities. If you're currently single, a cluttered bedroom limits your chances of finding and keeping a new partner.

For most people, the main problem in their bedroom is hanging on to clothes, shoes, and other items they'll never wear again. Go through your wardrobe carefully, and you'll find many items that you can discard or give away. This allows the ch'i more room in which to flow.

Many people store objects under the bed or on top of the wardrobe. The vanity is not intended to be a storage place for cosmetics. Once you've eliminated the clutter in these areas, you'll find yourself sleeping better, and you'll also find yourself luckier in all areas of life, especially your love life.

184. The Bed

It's considered lucky to position your bed on a north-south axis, but only if the bedroom allows you to do this naturally. This placement is also said to be lucky if you're wanting sons.

The foot of the bed should not face the doorway. This is known as the coffin position, because corpses are taken out feet first. Consequently, this is an unlucky position.

It's good luck for the head of the bed to be against a wall. This provides symbolic support for the bed.

The long side of the bed should not be placed against a wall unless you want to discourage potential partners. If you want to attract a partner, there should be sufficient space on each side of the bed for both you and your partner.

People lying in bed should be able to see the main entrance to the room without turning their heads more than 45 degrees. This provides a sense of security.

If a visitor has stayed overnight, you should not make the bed he or she slept in for at least an hour after your guest has left. This preserves and protects your good luck.

You should finish making the bed once you've started, as it's bad luck to leave the task half finished and return to complete it later. It's also unlucky to sneeze while making the bed, but this can be remedied by making the sign of the cross.

185. Getting Out of Bed

An old superstition says that when you get out of bed in the morning, you should put your right leg out first. This ensures harmonious relations with everyone you meet during the day. Consequently, the day will be pleasant, and good luck will flow your way. If you put your left leg out first, you'll experience difficulties and frustrations all day long.

186. The Home Office

A home office should be kept free of clutter, as this area relates to the family's wealth, status, and level of success. Anything that impedes the flow of ch'i will have a constricting effect on all of these.

Consequently, a stack of old catalogs, filing cabinets that are filled to overflowing, piles of papers on your desk, and boxes of computer paper on the floor all have the potential to hit you in the wallet. Your office should be a pleasant, comfortable environment where you can work without having to constantly search for everything you need.

Removing clutter from this room will increase your prosperity, as well as your luck.

187. Sweeping

Tradition says that when you're sweeping your house, you should always sweep the dust inwards. If you sweep it outwards, and out the door, all your luck will leave with it. It's perfectly acceptable to gather the dust into a container and take it outdoors that way.

The link between household dust and good luck and prosperity is hundreds of years old. In 1323, an Irish witch named Alice Kyteler was charged with trying to rob her fellow citizens of Kilkenny by sweeping the dust in front of their doors. By doing this she hoped to gain good luck and financial advantage for her and her son.[2]

There is one exception to this. An old superstition says that the first time a new broom is used, it should sweep something into the house, as this symbolically sweeps in good luck as well.

188. Flowers

The ancient Egyptians gave each other flowers as gestures of love and friendship. This beautiful tradition still exists today, and it has improved over the years as flowers are now also believed to provide good luck. The good luck increases if there are an odd number of flowers in the bunch.

Yellow flowers are said to be the best for providing good luck in the home. Purple flowers are useful, too, as they provide opportunities for financial progress as well as good luck.

189. Moving House

The luckiest days to move house are said to be Mondays and Wednesdays. An old superstition says that Saturday is the worst day to move house. You'll find it hard to settle in, and will move again quickly. The Pennsylvania Dutch thought Friday was the worst day to move house. They even have a saying for this: "Friday flitting means short sitting." This means you won't be living in that house for very long.

There are a number of superstitions concerned with bringing good luck into your new home. One of these recommends taking the embers from your old fireplace, and using them to kindle the fire in your new home. This preserves the good luck of the entire family. Interestingly, housewarming parties are derived from this, and it is a practice that enables friends to share in the family's good fortune.

It's also good luck to send a new broom to your new home before you move in. However, you should never move an old broom from one house to another.

You should carry a bucket of coal and a container of salt into your new home before bringing in any of your belongings. This is a gift for the home, and ensures it will prove lucky for you.

190. Housewarming

A housewarming party attracts good luck to the home and everyone who lives in it. Nowadays, a housewarming is an opportunity to entertain your friends and show off your new home. Traditionally, it was done to honor and thank the spirits that lived in the house.

The center of the home has always been the hearth, and the fire that was kept burning there was sacred. The ancient Greeks and Romans believed house gods worshiped at the hearth. Gradually, the house gods were replaced by a variety of fairies and other spirits who had to be honored and looked after to ensure the house received its share of prosperity and good luck. This is why the hearth and the grate had to be tidied up before the occupants went to bed. When people moved from one house to another, they would take live embers with them to start a fire in the new hearth. This was a "housewarming." By doing this, the family took their household spirits with them, and continued their good luck.

Eight

....

Seasons, Days, Months, and Years

Introduction

People have always been fascinated with time, and many methods have been devised to part the veil and gain a glimpse into the future. Because people's lifespans varied so enormously, good luck was credited with enabling some people to reach a ripe old age, while bad luck was blamed for causing some people to die young.

As human time is finite (compared to divine time, which is infinite), people designed special events, such as feasts and festivals, to try to temporarily escape the bonds of time. Charles Baudelaire (1821–1867), the French poet, wrote that time was "the watchful deadly foe, the enemy who gnaws at our hearts."

In this chapter are suggestions for every day of the week and month of the year. You can increase your opportunities for luck by acting on the traditional associations for these. You might want to start a creative hobby on a Wednesday or set yourself some goals on a Sunday. There's no reason why you can't do these things on any other day of the week, but if you have a choice in the matter, you should experiment and see if doing something at the traditional time associated with it helps matters go your way.

Special days such as birthdays and weddings are considered lucky by most people. However, there's no reason why you can't make any other day you wish a lucky one. All you need do is decide that on such-and-such a day, everything will go your way. Focus on the positive, and don't let anything disrupt your good mood. Be proactive, remain alert for opportunities, and see what happens. You'll discover you can make any day a lucky one by changing your attitude and expectations.

Seasonal Correspondences

There are traditional correspondences or associations with different seasons of the year. The objects associated with the season you were born in may well prove lucky for you.

191. Spring

Colors: yellow, white, pale green

Crystals: aventurine, jade, rose quartz

Flowers: crocus, daffodil, narcissus, snowdrop

In springtime—or if you want to capture the spirit of the season—carry a crystal that relates to spring, or wear something that contains some yellow, white, or pale green. Allow the energy of spring to make you feel positive about your life and future.

192. Summer

Colors: gold, orange, lilac, pink, red, purple, green

Crystals: amber, carnelian, citrine

Flowers: bluebell, foxglove, lilac, rose, sunflower

In summer, wear one of the colors that relates to summer, or carry a piece of amber, carnelian, or citrine with you to attract good luck. By doing this, you'll tap into the warmth and expansiveness of summer and will enjoy a positive, productive, and lucky day.

193. Fall/Autumn

Colors: blue, bronze, brown, gold

Crystals: amethyst, celestite, tiger's-eye

Flowers: chrysanthemum

As summer ends and winter draws near, wear something that contains blue, bronze, brown, or gold, or carry one of the crystals that relates to autumn with you to enhance your opportunities for good luck. You'll also feel more aware of the energy created by what is many people's favorite season.

194. Winter

Colors: black, gray, gold, dark green, silver, red

Crystals: clear quartz, smoky quartz, opal

Flowers: Christmas rose, poinsettia

Tune into the energies of winter by wearing one of the colors associated with the season, or you can carry a piece of clear or smoky quartz or opal with you. Winter is a good time for thinking ahead and making plans for the future.

Days of the Week

Every day is a lucky day for something. Luck is more likely to go your way if you focus your energies on whatever it is you desire on the correct day for your desire.

195. Monday

Monday relates to the moon. It's a lucky day for anything involving the immediate family, home, pets, women, emotions, and intuition. You can increase your luck on a Monday by wearing pearls.

196. Tuesday

Tuesday relates to the planet Mars. It's a lucky day for anything involving work, career, business, self-esteem, courage, and men. It's the perfect day for standing up for yourself and saying exactly what you feel. You can increase your luck on a Tuesday by wearing rubies.

197. Wednesday

Wednesday relates to Mercury. It's a lucky day for anything involving communication, creativity, and mental stimulation. Consequently, it's a good day to express yourself in some sort of way. This includes singing, talking, writing, and engaging in a creative interest. You can increase your luck on a Wednesday by wearing sapphires.

198. Thursday

Thursday relates to Jupiter. It's a lucky day for anything involving money, financial matters, prosperity, and travel. It's the perfect day to make plans relating to any of these. It's also a good day to start any challenging tasks. You can increase your luck on a Thursday by wearing garnets.

199. Friday

Friday relates to Venus. It's a lucky day for anything involving friendship, love, and social activities. All forms of entertainment and pleasure are enhanced on a Friday. You can increase your luck on a Friday by wearing emeralds.

200. Saturday

Saturday relates to Saturn. It's a lucky day for anything involving personal finances and protection. It's also a lucky day for eliminating negative emotions and feelings and expressing a more positive outlook on life. You can increase your luck on a Saturday by wearing diamonds.

201. Sunday

Sunday relates to the sun. It's the most favorable day of the week, and is a lucky day for anything involving self-worth, goal-setting, and anything personally important to you. You can increase your luck on a Sunday by wearing yellow stones.

202. Shrove Tuesday

Shrove Tuesday is the last day before Lent in the Christian calendar. It's often called "Pancake Day," as pancakes are traditionally prepared and eaten on this day to ensure good luck for the next twelve months. To ensure good luck, the pancakes need to be eaten before eight o'clock in the evening. Lent used to be a rather austere time of year, and Pancake Day was the last chance people had to enjoy themselves until after Easter.

Lucky Months

The luckiest months are those in which the last working day of the month is a Friday. It is almost as lucky if the first working day of the month is a Monday.

In addition to this, the luckiest month of the year for you is the one in which you were born.

203. January

January can be a lucky month if you focus on creating new ideas, start something new, or accept a leadership role. It's an excellent month for making changes and taking up new interests.

January is a good month to explore anything that is new or different. It's a good time to read a book on a subject you know nothing about, or perhaps have a conversation with someone who is an expert on a particular subject.

Even if the topic is only of passing interest, you'll learn something that might prove useful to you later.

204. February

February is a good month for cooperating with others, taking care of details, and making future plans. You will need to be patient, as matters will proceed more slowly than you would like. It's a lucky month for all close relationships.

205. March

March provides good opportunities for social activities, entertainment, and self-expression. It's a good month for travel and vacation. It's a lucky month for people engaged in creative activities.

206. April

April is a lucky month for people who are willing to work hard, and take advantage of the opportunities that present themselves. You need to take care of the details and be responsible and as organized as possible.

April, June, and November are traditionally the luckiest months to get married in.

207. May

May is a lucky month for making changes, exploring new ideas, and meeting new people. It's a time to expand your horizons and see the world from a different point of view. It's a good month for unexpected, lucky opportunities to present themselves.

208. June

June is a lucky month for anything involving loved ones, home, and family. The best opportunities appear when you put other people's needs ahead of your own. This is a particularly lucky month for love and romance.

According to tradition, June is the luckiest month to get married in. April and November are also considered lucky months for marriage.

209. July

July provides opportunities for inner growth and spiritual awakening. It's a good time for study and research. Lucky opportunities will come in quiet, contemplative moments when you are reevaluating the past, and looking ahead.

210. August

August was named after Emperor Augustus, who was the first Roman emperor. He considered it his lucky month, as he received his first consulship in August.

August is a lucky month as long as you're prepared to seize opportunities and act decisively. Opportunities for recognition, advancement, and financial benefit should all be taken advantage of, as luck is on your side.

211. September

September provides opportunities to help others, and to finish anything that has reached a natural conclusion. It's a lucky month for dealing with others, as long as you remain compassionate, kind, and understanding.

212. October

October is a good month for moving ahead. You should evaluate opportunities carefully and seize the ones that offer the most potential. Luck will be with you as long as you emphasize your individuality, originality, and ability to deal with others.

213. November

November can be a lucky month as long as you are prepared to be patient and wait for developments to progress. It's a time to cooperate with others, gather information, and be prepared to act when the time is right.

November, April, and June are all considered to be the luckiest months of the year to get married in.

214. December

December provides opportunities for fun and enjoyment. Luck will come through social activities and conversations with friends. As long as you remain positive and upbeat, everything will go your way.

215. Leap Years

Leap years are lucky years that favor changes and new undertakings. It's the best year to change career, start a business, move home, travel abroad, or do anything that takes you out of your comfort zone.

Not surprisingly, the luckiest day of the year on which to start anything is February 29.

216. Today's Lucky Number

Leap years occur only once every four years. However, you have a lucky number you can use today. The first step is to add up your day of birth, month of birth, and the current year, and reduce the total to a single digit. This creates what numerologists call your personal year number. If, for instance, you were born on August 23, and the year is 2015, you'd add up 8 (month) + 2 + 3 (day) + 2 + 0 + 1 + 5 (year) = 21, and as 2 + 1 = 3, your personal year number in 2015 would be 3.

The second step is to add your personal year number to the calendar day and month, and again reduce the total to a single digit. If today was March 17, 2015, you would add 3 (calendar month) + 1 + 7 (calendar day) + 3 (personal year) = 14, and 1 + 4 = 5. Your lucky number for March 17, 2015 is 5. You can work out your lucky number for any day using this formula.

— Part Four —

*Luck Throvghout
Cultvre and History*

Throughout history, people have searched for luck in many different ways. Some of their methods have become part of folklore. There can be few people in the Western world, for instance, who haven't heard that a four-leaf clover will attract good luck. Different cultures have developed their own particular ways to attract luck. Some techniques have stood the test of time, while others fell into disuse and have been forgotten. In this section we'll look at lucky animals, foods, the Chinese concept of luck, and the most popular folklore suggestions on how to attract luck and good fortune.

Nine

....

Lucky Animals

Introduction

Throughout human history, different cultures have associated luck with certain animals. Most of this came about from observing their behavior in their natural habitats, and noticing that certain animals appeared to be luckier than others. Some were resourceful, others were cunning, and others seemed to have a sixth sense about impending danger. Thousands of years ago, people began wearing items from certain animals believing they would provide them with luck. Many people still do this today, though usually they wear something depicting the animal, rather than an actual tooth or claw belonging to their lucky animal.

Many people collect ornaments that depict their favorite animal. They make an attractive display and provide their owners with hours of pleasure as they search for new specimens to add to their collections. Ornaments can also act as a source of good luck, if the owner believes this to be the case. My mother collected ceramic chickens on baskets, as she believed they provided her with good luck and abundance.

Instead of collecting objects that depict your favorite animal, you might look for examples of the animal everywhere you go. This is easy if your lucky animal happens to be a cat or dog. It might not be quite so easy if your animal is an anteater or an exotic bird, for example. If you seldom have the opportunity to see your lucky animal, you might carry a photograph of it with you. Alternatively, you might display a framed picture of your lucky animal in your home. Each time you see it, remind yourself that it's a symbol of good luck. Because all of these things encourage you to think of luck, you'll start looking for lucky opportunities in everything you do, and you'll notice that good fortune is smiling on you.

217. White Animals

White animals have been considered lucky for thousands of years. In ancient Rome, a lucky person was called "son of a white hen."

White rabbits have always been considered lucky in the United Kingdom. Many people around the world (including me) say "white rabbits" as soon as they wake up on the first of every month. This is supposed to provide good luck for the whole month. A friend told me that some people say "bunny, bunny, bunny" instead.

It's good luck to see a white horse, and even better to own one. Although the term "white elephant" is used to describe something useless or unworkable, white elephants are revered in many parts of Asia. They are said to bring good luck with them everywhere they go. If the first butterfly you see in the new year is a white one, you'll experience good luck all year.

218. Bear

The bear is considered lucky because it is able to survive the long winter months by hibernating. In Scandinavia, many people believe that bears are incarnations of the god Odin. As female bears are good mothers, bears symbolize good luck in home and family matters.

219. Bee

Bees are considered messengers of good luck. If a bee enters your home, it's a sign that good luck is coming your way. If possible, allow the bee to find its own way outdoors again. If it gets stuck behind a window you may have to help, but it's considered best if the bee flies in and out on its own.

If a bee lands on one of your hands, it's a sign of money in the near future. If it lands on your head, it's a sign that you have the potential to become famous.

Tradition says that when a beekeeper dies, the bees will attend the funeral. Beekeepers can improve their luck by telling their bees about everything that is occurring in their home and family lives.

220. Bird

Some birds are considered lucky, others are not. Blackbirds, doves, ducks, hummingbirds, kingfishers, martins, robins, storks, swallows, woodpeckers, and wrens are examples of birds that bring good luck. Blue and red birds are all considered lucky. The humble sparrow is considered lucky in some parts of the world, and unlucky in others. All around the world it's considered bad luck to kill one.

Although it may not be appreciated at the time, it's a sign of good luck coming your way if bird droppings land on your head.

221. Bull

The bull symbolizes virility and strength. The ancient Greeks wore pendants depicting bulls as symbols of fertility and good luck. The only personal experience I've had with a bull was being chased by one when I was about thirteen. I was relieved to get out of the field alive, and I still vividly remember the power, speed, and aggression the bull displayed.

222. Butterfly

The butterfly is a symbol of transformation, reincarnation, immortality, and the soul. Good luck is on its way if you see three butterflies fluttering together. In China, a butterfly is a sign of good luck in love.

223. Cardinal

If you happen to see a cardinal, also known as a redbird, you're assured of good luck in the near future. This luck is compounded if you blow a kiss at a sitting cardinal before it flies away.

224. Cat

The cat is a symbol of independence. Cats have been considered harbingers of both good and bad luck. Cats were worshiped in ancient Egypt, as they symbolized Bast, the goddess of the moon. Cats gradually developed a bad reputation as they could see in the dark, when evil spirits were around. People believed witches could transform themselves into black cats.

Nowadays, it's a sign of good luck for a stray black cat to walk into your home. Allow it to leave when it's ready. If you chase it out of the house, it will take your good luck with it. King Charles I had a black cat, and when it died he said his luck was gone. One day later he was arrested.

It's good luck to go for a walk and find a cat on your right side. It's good luck for your finances if this cat crosses your path and continues to the left. It's also a sign of good luck if your cat sneezes in the morning. Three sneezes in a row at any time of day is a sign of good luck. It's extremely good luck for a cat to sneeze near a bride on her wedding day.

A cat can also be used to symbolically increase the number of guests if you happen to have thirteen people sitting down for dinner. People who have a fear of the number thirteen can then relax, as the cat increases the total to fourteen.

225. Cricket

Hearing the chirp of a cricket is a sign of good luck. Killing a cricket is said to bring bad luck. In Japan, people keep crickets in tiny bamboo cages as good luck charms. They have been doing this since at least the tenth century. In Barbados, a cricket chirping inside the house is a sign that money is coming. In Zambia, seeing a cricket is considered a sign of good luck. It's a sign of good luck coming your way for crickets to come into your home.

226. Cuckoo

The cuckoo is an interesting bird as it can be both lucky and unlucky. Traditionally, the cuckoo is the harbinger of spring. It's unlucky to hear the first cuckoo of spring before April 6. However, it's extremely lucky if you hear a cuckoo for the first time on April 28.

It's also lucky if this first call comes from in front of you or from your right. However, it's said to be bad luck if you hear it behind you, or from your left side.

Folklore says that no matter when or from where you hear the first cuckoo of spring, you should turn over the money in your pocket while making a wish. The wish will be granted and you'll enjoy good luck.

227. Deer

Deer symbolize gentleness, gracefulness, and beauty. The Chinese consider the deer lucky as the Chinese word for deer, *lu*, is a homophone and also means "income." As they also consider the deer a symbol of longevity, in China a deer means a long and prosperous life.

228. Dog

The dog symbolizes loyalty, friendship, and unconditional love. It's also considered "man's best friend." It's a sign that good luck is coming your way if you're followed by a stray dog. It's also a lucky sign if a dog walks into your home. If the dog is golden, your fortunes will increase. A white dog is a sign of romance, and a black dog provides protection.

One dog in particular is considered a sign of good luck. This is the Tibetan Terrier, or Tsang Apso ("shaggy dog from the province of Tsang"). The Tibetan Terrier is the holy dog of Tibet, and no one who owned one would ever sell it, although it could be given as a gift. This is because these dogs are considered emblems of good luck, and no one would willingly sell their good luck. Tibetan Terriers were considered part of the family, and were treated extremely well. Mistreating one brought bad luck to the entire community. Tibetan Terriers were not seen in Europe until the 1920s when a Tibetan nobleman presented one to a British doctor who had treated his ill wife. These dogs were introduced to the United States in 1957. They are often called "luck bearers" or "luck bringers."

229. Donkey

The donkey is considered a lucky animal, as the dark hairs across its shoulders form the shape of a cross. People used to believe that these hairs appeared only after a donkey had carried Jesus Christ into Jerusalem. Superstitious people used to pluck three of these hairs as they believed they were able to cure a variety of illnesses. In the Christian tradition, donkeys are considered a symbol of patience and humility.

It is said that if a pregnant woman sees a donkey, her unborn child will grow up to be intelligent, well behaved, and lucky. Farmers sometimes keep donkeys with their cows to protect the luck of the herd. They are said to prevent accidents and premature births.

230. Dragonfly

Dragonflies are considered lucky as they're associated with change and transformation. Its agility, speed, and ability to fly in all directions, including backwards, led people to believe it possessed maturity and insight. Consequently, it's always been considered a sign of good luck to see one.

231. Elephant

Elephants are considered lucky because of their intelligence, strength, wisdom, loyalty, and longevity. They are also considered symbols of power and prosperity.

In India, Ganesh the elephant god removes obstacles and brings good luck.

232. Fox

Foxes are renowned for their boldness, craftiness, and cunning ways. The Welsh people have a saying that it's lucky to see one fox, but unlucky to see many. In ancient Egypt, foxes were said to carry favors from the gods.

233. Frog

In Japan, frogs are a symbol of good luck. They also represent transformation, as they change from tadpoles into frogs. The story of the frog prince also shows this as the frog is transformed back into a prince. Frogs also symbolize abundance, because of the large number of eggs they lay. They are also reputed to protect young children. It's a sign of good luck if a frog comes into your garden. If you make a wish when you see your first frog in spring, it will come true.

234. Goldfish

The goldfish is a symbol of tranquillity, happiness, longevity, and good luck. The ancient Egyptians believed goldfish ensured good luck for the family.

The ancient Greeks believed they brought luck into all relationships, especially marriage. In the Christian tradition, fish are a sign of abundance as Jesus fed five thousand people with five loaves of bread and two fishes.

235. Horse

Horses are considered special, magical animals that provide good fortune. They symbolize stamina, power, and loyalty. Every part of a horse is believed to be lucky, but horseshoes are considered the luckiest.

236. Pig

The pig symbolizes fertility, shrewdness, intelligence, and prosperity. Of course, it also symbolizes gluttony, greed, and lust. The pig is considered a lucky animal in both China and Ireland. In China, the pig is said to provide good luck for anyone who is self-employed.

237. Rabbit

Rabbits are considered lucky for many reasons. Rabbits are extremely fertile, and people used to believe their babies were born with their eyes open. Because of this, people thought rabbits could ward off the evil eye. Rabbits burrowed into the earth, and in the past, people were scared of darkness and what lay under the ground. Rabbits are also extremely fast, thanks to their powerful rear legs. Because of this, the rabbit's foot became (and remains) one of the most popular of all good luck charms.

238. Sheep

Sheep are considered lucky animals in Christian countries as they're associated with the Good Shepherd. Some people think sheep remember the Nativity, and face east and bow their heads at midnight on Christmas Eve.

It's a sign of good luck to see a flock of sheep on a country road. It's even better luck to walk or drive carefully through them. This belief dates back to the days when people lived in small, isolated communities. The sight of a shepherd and his flock meant that fresh meat and wool would be available.

Lambs are also lucky, especially when you see your first one in spring. Your wish will be granted if you make it immediately after seeing a black lamb.

239. Spider

Spiders have always been considered a sign of persistence and prosperity. In the United Kingdom, small spiders are sometimes referred to as money-spinners, and it's a sure sign of money coming your way if one lands near you. Finding a spider on your clothing is a sign that you'll soon be wearing new clothes. If you find your initials in a spider's web, you'll enjoy good luck forever.

It's bad luck to kill a spider. There's an old saying that relates to this:

If you want to live and thrive,
Let the spider run alive.

240. Stork

Storks are traditionally considered bringers of good luck. In ancient Egypt, the stork was associated with the soul. In ancient Greece and Rome, storks were considered symbols of family values and love. According to European folklore, it is storks that bring babies to the new parents. Even today, many children are told that the stork brought them when they ask where they came from. At one time, storks were believed to look after their aged parents as well as their own children. Because of this, they are associated with home and family.

In Germany and the Netherlands, people encourage storks to nest on the roofs of their homes, as they believe this will provide good luck for the whole family. As storks can live up to seventy years, once you've successfully encouraged storks to nest on your home, they'll keep returning for many years.

241. Swallow

As swallows are harbingers of spring, people are always pleased to see them. However, you need to see a number of them before concluding that summer has arrived. The old saying "one swallow doesn't make a summer" refers to this. Swallows symbolize hope, fertility, and—as they are monogamous—a happy home and family life. It's a sign of good luck for the whole family if a swallow chooses to build a nest on your house. The luckiest place for the nest is in the eaves. It's bad luck if a swallow builds a nest, but then leaves it unexpectedly. It's bad luck to kill a swallow or to destroy its nest.

Seeing a swallow in flight is also a sign of good luck.

Ten

....

Food and Drink

Introduction

Food and drink have always been associated with luck. Primitive man thought that by eating the flesh or organ of a particular animal, he'd gain some of their desirable qualities. If he ate the heart of a lion, for instance, he'd gain the strength of a lion. In the extreme, cannibals believed they'd gain courage and strength by eating the bodies of their slain enemies. Foods such as oysters that are believed to possess aphrodisiacal qualities are regularly eaten in the hope of providing good luck in the bedroom.

People raise their glasses to make a toast, which is a ritual intended to celebrate an occasion, honor someone, or make a wish for good luck.

A friend of mine eats a couple of pieces of dark chocolate every evening. He started doing this to reward himself whenever he had an especially productive day. However, he started eating it every day when he noticed that the chocolate appeared to give him good luck. It doesn't matter if this is true or not. My friend thinks dark chocolate makes him lucky, and because he believes this, it works for him.

If you intend using a specific food or drink to attract good luck, tell yourself that you're creating good luck each time you partake of it.

242. Salt

As salt is cheap and plentiful today we barely give it a moment's thought. However, in the past it was rare and valuable. If someone says, "You're worth your salt," you know that you're valued. An allowance of salt was made to officers and men in the Roman army. In imperial times, this *salarium* became a payment that was used to buy salt.[1] The word "salary" comes from this. Salt is also an excellent preservative, and became associated with good health and longevity. Because it prevented decay, it became associated with immortality and was used in magical rituals. This is why it's considered lucky.

It's considered unlucky to borrow salt. It's certainly unlucky to spill it, a belief that dates back to the days when it was rare and expensive. There's even a legend that says Judas spilled the salt before betraying Jesus. Leonardo da Vinci depicted this in his painting, *The Last Supper*. A number of remedies have been devised to counteract the bad luck that occurs when salt is spilt. The most common remedy is to immediately throw a pinch of salt over your left shoulder. Alternatively, you can drop a few grains into the fire or onto the stove.

243. Tomato

The tomato is native to parts of South and Central America. Hernán Cortéz (1485–1547), the Spanish conqueror of Mexico, allegedly found them growing in the gardens of the Aztec Emperor Montezuma in 1519, and took seeds back to Europe with him. People grew tomatoes for ornamental purposes, but did not eat them. Initially, people were wary of them, as the acid in tomatoes caused lead to leech out of pewter flatware causing lead poisoning. The French botanist Joseph Pitton de Tournefort (1656–1708) did not help matters either, by giving tomatoes the botanical name *Lycopersicon esculentum*, which means "wolf peach." He erroneously associated the tomato with the wolf peach mentioned by Galen in the third century. Galen claimed the wolf peach was poisonous and killed wolves. It was not until the early twentieth century that tomatoes became popular as a food in America.

In France, as in most of Europe, the tomato was considered a decorative plant until the time of the French Revolution. As the French called the tomato *pomme d'amour* (love apple), the tomato gained a reputation for being an aphrodisiac, and virgins refused to eat it until after they were married.

In Italy, the tomato has enjoyed a good reputation for at least two hundred years. A red tomato sitting in a window wards off evil spirits, while another placed on the mantelpiece attracts wealth and abundance. Tomato sauce provides prosperity and good health. Because of this, anything shaped like a tomato is said to attract good luck. My grandmother had a pincushion in the shape of a tomato. We used to enjoy pushing pins into it, as she told us it would bring us good luck.

244. Coin-Like Foods

Foods that look like coins are said to provide good luck. Peas, grapes, oranges, round cookies, and even round donuts are good examples.

Black-eyed peas are an excellent example, as they were eaten to provide good luck at Rosh Hashana, the Jewish New Year, more than fifteen hundred years ago. In the south of the United States, black-eyed peas are served in a peas-and-rice dish called hoppin' John on New Year's Day to provide good luck and prosperity for the next twelve months. This tradition dates back to the Civil War.

In Italy, lentils are said to provide good luck, especially in money matters. The more of them you eat, the luckier you'll become.

245. Green Vegetables

Children (and many adults) are constantly told to eat more greens. In fact, many people eat greens because the color reminds them of folding currency, and this makes them think of wealth and prosperity. They believe that eating greens makes them luckier financially. This is a useful superstition, as most of us need to eat more "greens."

246. Pork

Eating pork is said to provide good luck. This is because pigs root forward, indicating continued forward progress. In addition, the rotundness of a pig symbolizes prosperity and enjoyment of the good things in life.

In Italy, the fatty meat symbolizes a fattening wallet. Pork is a popular meat in Italy all year round, but it is eaten for good luck on New Year's Day.

247. Fish

Fish are considered lucky for three main reasons: their scales are round and symbolize money, they swim in schools, which symbolize prosperity, and they swim forward, a sign of forward progress.

In China, fish are considered silent affirmations that symbolize upward progress. This came about when people observed carp swimming against the currents, and leaping up waterfalls to get to their breeding grounds. The carp is an ancient Chinese and Japanese symbol of endurance and perseverance that was used to motivate young men. People used to believe that once a carp became a hundred years old, it could swim up a river, leap over the Dragon Gate, and become a dragon, one of the most auspicious symbols in all Asia. Since the tenth century, the Japanese have used carp-shaped banners in their Boys' Day Festival (now known as Childrens' Festival), known as the Feast of Flags. In China, the carp signifies passing examinations, especially the Civil Service exams, which provide the potential for a successful career. As carp are also associated with the god of literature, they are used to encourage success in literary exams.

Raw carp is eaten during the Chinese New Year to attract luck into the home. Everyone in the family takes turns to stir the dish of carp, spices, oils, and wine to ensure a happy new year for every member of the household. The best day to eat this dish is on the seventh day of the Chinese New Year. In addition to this, the Chinese name for carp, *lei yu*, sounds like "have wealth." For this reason, the carp symbolizes wealth, ambition, and good luck.

Goldfish are considered symbols of wealth and abundance in China. Two goldfish swimming together symbolize a happy marriage, and nine fish symbolize wealth. Fish ornaments are worn to avert evil and attract good luck.

248. Tea and Coffee

If you need some good luck, folklore suggests you use a spoon to capture the bubbles on the surface of a cup of tea or coffee. If you drink these before the bubbles break, you'll attract good luck for the rest of the day.

249. Noodles

Noodles are a staple of the Asian diet. However, in many parts of Asia, especially long noodles are eaten on New Year's Day to encourage good luck and a long life. It's important that the noodles aren't cut before boiling and that they are unbroken until they are all in your mouth.

250. Mince Pie

The term "mince pie" has different meanings in different countries. In some places it is a variety of meat pie, but for the purposes of luck I'm referring to a fruit mince pie, sometimes called a Christmas mince tart.

It's good luck to be offered a mince pie. Consequently, you should never decline the offer, even if you have just eaten a number of them. If possible, eat a mince pie on each of the twelve days of Christmas. Each pie gives you a month of good luck.

251. Sugar

Sugar may not be good for our health, but it is considered lucky. You can attract good luck by dropping a few grains of sugar on the ground in any environment where you feel you need more luck. If, for instance, you were going to be interviewed for a job that you really wanted, you could carry a small amount of sugar in a pocket and drop a few grains as you walk through the lobby of the building. You might drop a few more in the office where you are being interviewed.

It's important to use only a few grains. There's no need to leave a spoonful of sugar everywhere you go. A few grains will not be noticed by anyone, but a larger amount might, and that could attract bad luck—not to mention certain pests—rather than good.

252. Christmas Pudding

In the past, all families made their own Christmas puddings. This is less common nowadays, which is unfortunate, as it brings luck to the family. Every member of the family should have a turn at stirring the mixture while making a wish. The pudding should be stirred clockwise, and the wishes need to be kept secret.

Sometimes silver coins were added to the mixture to provide financial good luck over the next twelve months. A ring was also sometimes mixed in to encourage a wedding to take place.

Eleven

....

Luck in the Far East

Introduction

People in Asia enjoy surrounding themselves with objects that they think will bring good luck their way. The Chinese have three important gods, Fu, Lu, and Shou, that are usually depicted together. Fu is the god of luck, Lu is the god of prosperity, and Shou is the god of longevity.

The Chinese character for *fu* is a popular decoration, and is usually displayed upside down. This is because the Chinese word for "arrived," *dao*, sounds exactly the same as the phrase "to turn upside down." Consequently, when the lucky character is hung upside down, it means "luck has arrived."

The Chinese have charming stories for almost everything, and the figure for fu is no exception. Apparently, one of Prince Gong's officials asked his servants to paste some large fu characters on the doors leading into the palace and storerooms. One of them accidentally pasted his characters upside down. Prince Gong was furious when he saw this, and demanded that the culprit be found and punished. The official, perhaps worried about being punished himself, quickly explained that an upside-down fu was extremely lucky, as it meant that good luck had arrived. The prince was delighted when he heard this, and instead of punishing the servant, he gave all the servants fifty taels of silver.

People in Asia take the concepts of luck and fate seriously. A person's destiny is dictated by the day and time of his or her birth. However, this can be modified by the person's environment, character, level of education, and willingness to make the required amount of effort.

If you decide to experiment with some of the suggestions in this chapter, you must be prepared to accompany them with effort. If you simply wait for luck to occur, it will pass you by.

253. Bat

The bat is a symbol of good luck because the word for bat, *biān fu*, is similar to fu, the word for luck. Two bats facing each other symbolize "twice the luck." A picture of a red bat is extremely lucky as in the East red repels evil. A bat next to a coin means "luck before your eyes."

Five bats are extremely propitious as they equate to the "five good fortunes" of longevity, wealth, health, love of virtue, and a natural death. This is sometimes expressed as a wish: "May the five fortunes come to your door."

254. Dragon

The Chinese have four "spiritually endowed" creatures, together called the *si ling*. They are the dragon, phoenix, unicorn, and tortoise. They all attract good luck in different ways. The dragon in addition to being lucky, symbolizes strength, courage, endurance, and power. Images of dragons are displayed to attract good luck. The ultimate example of this can be found in the Forbidden City in Beijing where thousands of dragons are depicted on the walls, ceilings, doors, and furniture.

255. Phoenix

The phoenix symbolizes warmth, prosperity, the sun, and beauty. It provides good luck to couples who are wanting a family. Consequently, it is often found with the dragon in wedding ceremonies to wish the couple a long, happy, lucky life, with many descendants.

256. Unicorn

The unicorn is the third celestial creature. It symbolizes wisdom, longevity, peace, compassion, and goodwill. It provides good luck in the form of wisdom, long life, and successful children.

257. Tortoise

The tortoise symbolizes longevity, fortitude, and good health. The dragon, phoenix, and unicorn are mythical creatures, but the tortoise belongs to this group as at one time people believed it to be immortal. It provides good luck in the form of good health and a long life.

258. Lucky Children

Pictures of a chubby boy and girl are often attached to doors of homes and businesses. They are known as *da ah fu*, and they provide protection, happiness, and good luck. Originally, the two figures were made from clay, but today they are more commonly drawn on paper. Newlywed couples often display statues of da ah fu in their homes.

259. Money Sword

The traditional Chinese money sword, made of coins held together with red thread, has become a popular charm in the West thanks to the growing interest in feng shui. They were originally made in the belief that the emperors who were ruling when the coins were made would repel any evil spirits or ghosts. Money swords are usually hung over the head of the bed, but can be displayed anywhere. They are charms to attract prosperity and good luck.

260. Pinwheel

In China, handheld pinwheels are purchased and displayed during the Chinese New Year, as they are believed to increase the person's good luck in the upcoming year. Pinwheels are able to turn people's luck around and create good luck where there was little or no luck before. These pinwheels often contain a phrase that wishes the owner good luck, prosperity, or good health.

261. Chinese Astrology

In the East, Chinese astrology has been used for thousands of years to help people improve the quality of their lives. Luck plays an important part of this, and you can use the animal that relates to your year of birth to help improve your luck. Here are the animals that relate to each year:

+ Monkey—20 February 1920 to 7 February 1921

+ Rooster—8 February 1921 to 27 January 1922

+ Dog—28 January 1922 to 15 February 1923

+ Pig—16 February 1923 to 4 February 1924

+ Rat—5 February 1924 to 24 January 1925

+ Ox—25 January 1925 to 12 February 1926

+ Tiger—13 February 1926 to 1 February 1927

+ Rabbit—2 February 1927 to 22 January 1928

+ Dragon—23 January 1928 to 9 February 1929

+ Snake—10 February 1929 to 29 January 1930

+ Horse—30 January 1930 to 16 February 1931

- Goat—17 February 1931 to 5 February 1932

- Monkey—6 February 1932 to 25 January 1933

- Rooster—26 January 1933 to 13 February 1934

- Dog—14 February 1934 to 3 February 1935

- Pig—4 February 1935 to 23 January 1936

- Rat—24 January 1936 to 10 February 1937

- Ox—11 February 1937 to 30 January 1938

- Tiger—31 January 1938 to 18 February 1939

- Rabbit—19 February 1939 to 7 February 1940

- Dragon—8 February 1940 to 26 January 1941

- Snake—27 January 1941 to 14 February 1942

- Horse—15 February 1942 to 4 February 1943

- Goat—5 February 1943 to 24 January 1944

- Monkey—25 January 1944 to 12 February 1945

- Rooster—13 February 1945 to 1 February 1946

- Dog—2 February 1946 to 21 January 1947

- Pig—22 January 1947 to 9 February 1948

- Rat—10 February 1948 to 28 January 1949

- Ox—29 January 1949 to 16 February 1950

- Tiger—17 February 1950 to 5 February 1951

- Rabbit—6 February 1951 to 26 January 1952

- Dragon—27 January 1952 to 13 February 1953

- Snake—14 February 1953 to 2 February 1954

- Horse—3 February 1954 to 23 January 1955

- Goat—24 January 1955 to 11 February 1956

- Monkey—12 February 1956 to 30 January 1957

- Rooster—31 January 1957 to 17 February 1958

- Dog—18 February 1958 to 7 February 1959

- Pig—8 February 1959 to 27 January 1960

- Rat—28 January 1960 to 14 February 1961

- Ox—15 February 1961 to 4 February 1962

- Tiger—5 February 1962 to 24 January 1963

- Rabbit—25 January 1963 to 12 February 1964

- Dragon—13 February 1964 to 1 February 1965

- Snake—2 February 1965 to 20 January 1966

- Horse—21 January 1966 to 8 February 1967

- Goat—9 February 1967 to 29 January 1968

- Monkey—30 January 1968 to 16 February 1969

- Rooster—17 February 1969 to 5 February 1970

- Dog—6 February 1970 to 26 January 1971

- Pig—27 January 1971 to 14 February 1972

- Rat—15 February 1972 to 2 February 1973

- Ox—3 February 1973 to 22 January 1974

- Tiger—23 January 1974 to 10 February 1975

- Rabbit—11 February 1975 to 30 January 1976
- Dragon—31 January 1976 to 17 February 1977
- Snake—18 February 1977 to 6 February 1978
- Horse—7 February 1978 to 27 January 1979
- Goat—28 January 1979 to 15 February 1980
- Monkey—16 February 1980 to 4 February 1981
- Rooster—5 February 1981 to 24 January 1982
- Dog—25 January 1982 to 12 February 1983
- Pig—13 February 1983 to 1 February 1984
- Rat—2 February 1984 to 19 February 1985
- Ox—20 February 1985 to 8 February 1986
- Tiger—9 February 1986 to 28 January 1987
- Rabbit—29 January 1987 to 16 February 1988
- Dragon—17 February 1988 to 5 February 1989
- Snake—6 February 1989 to 26 January 1990
- Horse—27 January 1990 to 14 February 1991
- Goat—15 February 1991 to 3 February 1992
- Monkey—4 February 1992 to 22 January 1993
- Rooster—23 January 1993 to 9 February 1994
- Dog—10 February 1994 to 30 January 1995
- Pig—31 January 1995 to 18 February 1996
- Rat—19 February 1996 to 6 February 1997

- Ox—7 February 1997 to 27 January 1998
- Tiger—28 January 1998 to 15 February 1999
- Rabbit—16 February 1999 to 4 February 2000
- Dragon—5 February 2000 to 23 January 2001
- Snake—24 January 2001 to 11 February 2002
- Horse—12 February 2002 to 31 January 2003
- Goat—1 February 2003 to 21 January 2004
- Monkey—22 January 2004 to 8 February 2005
- Rooster—9 February 2005 to 28 January 2006
- Dog—29 January 2006 to 17 February 2007
- Pig—18 February 2007 to 6 February 2008
- Rat—7 February 2008 to 25 January 2009
- Ox—26 January 2009 to 13 February 2010
- Tiger—14 February 2010 to 2 February 2011
- Rabbit—3 February 2011 to 22 January 2012
- Dragon—23 January 2012 to 9 February 2013
- Snake—10 February 2013 to 30 January 2014
- Horse—31 January 2014 to 18 February 2015
- Goat—19 February 2015 to 7 February 2016
- Monkey—8 February 2016 to 27 January 2017
- Rooster—28 January 2017 to 15 February 2018

+ Dog—16 February 2018 to 4 February 2019

+ Pig—5 February 2019 to 24 January 2020

262. Astrological Luck

You can improve your luck by improving the ch'i of the area of your home that relates to your animal sign. Your luck will increase if you attract as much positive energy as possible into this part of your home. Unfortunately, you can't do this if you have a toilet or bathroom in this area of your home.

You can activate this area of your home with an attractive ornament of your particular animal sign. If possible, surround this image with gemstones and crystals. If you wish, you can also activate this direction in your office, and even on your desk.

Here are the compass directions for each sign:

+ Rat—352.5° to 7.5°

+ Ox—22.5° to 37.5°

+ Tiger—52.5° to 67.5°

+ Rabbit—82.5° to 97.5°

+ Dragon—112.5° to 127.5°

+ Snake—142.5° to 157.5°

+ Horse—172.5° to 187.5°

+ Goat—202.5° to 217.5°

+ Monkey—232.5° to 247.5°

+ Rooster—262.5° to 277.5°

+ Dog—292.5° to 307.5°

+ Pig—322.5° to 337.5°

263. Peach Blossom Luck

Peach blossom luck relates to love and romance. If you are trying to find the right partner, you can activate part of your home to attract the right person to you.

Peach Blossom Luck For Ox, Snake, and Rooster

If you were born in the year of the Ox, Snake, or Rooster and want to have more luck in love, you need to display an image or ornament of a horse in the south part of your home. This will activate your peach blossom luck, and help you find the right partner. Take your time choosing your horse, as it needs to be attractive and appealing. If the south part of your home is a bathroom, place the horse in the south part of your living room.

Peach Blossom Luck For Rat, Dragon, and Monkey

If you were born in the year of the Rat, Dragon, or Monkey and want to have more luck in love, you need to display a rooster in the west side of your home. If this area contains the bathroom, place the rooster in the west of your bedroom.

Peach Blossom Luck For Rabbit, Goat, and Pig

If you were born in the year of the Rabbit, Goat, or Pig and want to have more luck in love, you need to display an ornament of a rat in the north part of your home. The rat has negative connotations in the West, but in the East it is an emblem of ingenuity. If your bathroom is in the north, place the figurine in the north part of your living room.

Peach Blossom Luck For Tiger, Horse, and Dog

If you were born in the year of the Tiger, Horse, or Dog and want to have more luck in love, you need to display an ornament of a rabbit in the east part of your home. Place this in the east part of your living room if you have a bathroom in the east part of your home.

264. Plum Blossom Luck

Plum blossom luck works well in association with peach blossom luck. Plum blossom luck is used to encourage a permanent partner into your life.

Find at least one drawing, painting, or ornament that symbolizes love and marriage. Two or more would be even better. Ideally, at least one of the items should consist of a matching pair. A pair of doves, for instance, would be ideal. It's important that you choose items that you find attractive.

Display these items in the southwest corner of your home. Look after them. Keep them dusted, and talk to them at least once a day until the special person comes into your life.

265. Peony

The peony is the flower of spring. It's considered a symbol of honor, wealth, and good luck. It also symbolizes love and feminine beauty. When it is in full bloom, the peony is considered a sign of good luck and happiness. The peony is frequently depicted in Chinese art, enabling people to display a picture of peonies in full bloom all year round.

266. Chrysanthemum

The chrysanthemum is the flower of autumn. It symbolizes joy and happiness. However, its main symbolism is that it makes the path through life smoother and easier. This makes it a lucky flower. Displays of yellow chrysanthemums can be found at all Chinese festivals to create an atmosphere of happiness and cheerfulness.

267. Lotus

The lotus is the flower of summer, and is considered a sacred plant in China. It symbolizes purity, as it rises from water that is frequently murky and dirty to reveal its beautiful flower to the world. It is also a symbol of spirituality, peace, and leisure.

268. Magnolia

The magnolia symbolizes positive thinking, hopes, wishes, and dreams for the future. It also symbolizes feminine sweetness and beauty.

269. Orchid

The orchid symbolizes elegance and refinement. It is a flower of love and friendship, and also symbolizes virtue and high moral standards. It is a popular flower at Chinese weddings as it also a symbol of fertility and good luck.

270. Peach

In Chinese culture, the peach symbolizes immortality and the promise of eternal life. In Chinese legend, the god of immortality appeared from a peach. Paintings depicting this scene or showing the god holding a golden peach are popular gifts, especially to the older members of the family.

271. Orange

The orange symbolizes happiness, wealth, and good luck. At the time of the Chinese New Year, oranges are displayed in homes and given to others as gifts. Its association with wealth is derived partly because it is round and gold, and symbolizes a gold coin. It also comes from the fact that the Chinese words for "orange" and "gold"—*gan ju*—sound similar.

272. Pomegranate

As the pomegranate has many seeds, it symbolizes large families with many children, all of whom will be successful and provide honor to the family name. The pomegranate is one of the three fortunate fruits that provide abundance and wealth. The other two fruits are the peach and the lemon. A picture of a half-opened pomegranate is a popular gift at Chinese weddings.

273. Persimmon

The persimmon symbolizes joy, happiness, financial success, and good fortune. When the persimmon is combined with a tangerine, a special meaning is created: "May you have good fortune in all your undertakings." Not surprisingly, paintings of persimmons and tangerines make popular gifts.

274. Money Luck

Cut a twelve-inch length of green string and wind it five times around your little finger. Men should tie this around the little finger on their left hand; women should use the little finger on the right hand. The string should be wound around the finger in a clockwise direction with the fingers pointing away from you. Tie the string with a knot. Whenever the knot gets wet, replace the string. The string creates a ring that will attract good luck. This ring is used mainly to attract good luck in financial matters.

275. Your Lucky Friends

The twelve Chinese astrological signs are divided into three groups of four. People belonging to signs in the same group as you can be extremely beneficial, and bring you an endless supply of good luck. People belonging to three of the signs in your group will prove to be powerful allies, mentors, and confidantes. People belonging to the fourth sign will become "secret friends." A secret friend is someone whom you may not initially consider a friend, but who demonstrates through actions and conversations that, in fact, he or she is a true friend.

It's a sign of good luck if a person from any of the four signs in your group comes into your life. There is a formula to determine your allies and secret friend.

Your allies are four signs apart. The animal signs rotate in the following order:

1. Rat
2. Ox
3. Tiger
4. Rabbit
5. Dragon
6. Snake
7. Horse
8. Sheep
9. Monkey
10. Rooster
11. Dog
12. Pig

Following this chart, we can see that the Rat's allies are the Dragon and the Monkey, and the Rooster's allies are the Ox and the Snake.

The secret friend is worked out differently:

+ 9. Monkey, 8. Sheep, 7. Horse, 6. Snake,
+ 10. Rooster, 5. Dragon,
+ 11. Dog, 4. Rabbit,
+ 12. Pig, 1. Rat, 2. Ox, 3. Tiger.

In the first row, the Monkey and Snake are secret friends, as are the Sheep and the Horse.

In the second row, the Rooster and Dragon are secret friends.

In the third row, the Dog and Rabbit are secret friends.

In the fourth row, the Pig and Tiger are secret friends, as are the Rat and Ox.

Here are the animal signs, and the good luck signs for each one:

+ Rat—Dragon and Monkey. Secret friend: Ox.

+ Ox—Snake and Rooster. Secret friend: Rat.

+ Tiger—Horse and Dog. Secret friend: Pig.

+ Rabbit—Sheep and Pig. Secret friend: Dog.

+ Dragon—Rat and Monkey. Secret friend: Rooster.

+ Snake—Rooster and Ox. Secret friend: Monkey.

+ Horse—Tiger and Dog. Secret friend: Sheep.

+ Sheep—Rabbit and Pig. Secret friend: Horse.

+ Monkey—Dragon and Rat. Secret friend: Snake.

+ Rooster—Snake and Ox. Secret friend: Dragon.

+ Dog—Horse and Tiger. Secret friend: Rabbit.

+ Pig—Sheep and Rabbit. Secret friend: Tiger.

You can increase the luck aspect of your allies and secret friend by keeping ornaments or images of them in your home. You can also carry them on you as a charm bracelet consisting of four animals: your sign, plus your two allies and secret friend.

276. Fish and Your Career

Fish have been considered powerful symbols of good fortune and luck for thousands of years. The ancient Chinese watched carp leaping up waterfalls to reach the breeding grounds, and considered them symbols of upward progress.

You can use an aquarium to activate luck in your career. The aquarium should be placed in the north corner of your living room, or any other room where you spend much of your time. It's important that the aquarium is well looked after, and the water is circulated to prevent it from becoming stagnant. If the aquarium is large enough, you should have nine fish in it. Eight of these should be gold or red, while the ninth fish should be black. The black fish will absorb any bad luck that is coming your way. If a fish dies, it means it has absorbed bad luck, and should be replaced as quickly as possible.

277. The Horse and Your Career

In the East, the horse is a symbol of recognition, promotion, and increased status. Consequently, to activate your career, you might like to place an image of a horse in the south part of your living room or bedroom. This horse needs to be dusted and looked after. Some people believe that placing a monkey on the horse increases the potential for luck and prosperity.

278. Passion and Luck

Red is a stimulating color, and the Chinese use red peony flowers to reignite the passion that previously existed in long-term relationships. If you want more luck in the bedroom, introduce a bowl of peonies, or hang a picture of peonies on the wall.

As anything red will increase passion, look for attractive red objects that will fit in with your bedroom's decor, and enjoy the results they provide.

279. Four Lucky Fruits

Peaches, oranges, pomegranates, and persimmon are considered the four lucky (sometimes called "good fortune") fruits. They each symbolize different aspects of good luck.

The peach symbolizes marriage and immortality. The Chinese god of immortality is said to have emerged from a peach, and paintings of this god always show him carrying a peach.

The orange symbolizes prosperity, good fortune, and happiness. Its shape and color make people think of gold, and at the time of the Lunar New Year people display them in their homes, eat them, and give them away as gifts.

As the pomegranate has many seeds, it symbolizes large families, with many successful children.

The persimmon symbolizes friendship, happiness, joy, and good luck. It provides a smooth path through life.

280. Laughing Buddha

The Maitreya Buddha, better known in the West as the Laughing Buddha, is a chubby, laughing Buddha with a large stomach. He is usually ceramic, but is sometimes carved from jade, ivory, or wood. Seeing this Buddha every day should make you smile and feel happy. Even better, it's said that if you rub his stomach at least once a day you'll attract good luck.

281. Birthdays

Birthdays in China are always held on or before the actual day. It's bad luck to celebrate a birthday belatedly. Several birthdays are not celebrated, as they are potentially unlucky. For women, the uncelebrated birthdays are at the ages of thirty, thirty-three, and sixty-six. The year following these birthdays is believed to contain significant problems. Consequently, women in China remain twenty-nine for two years. Upon turning thirty-three, a woman would need to buy a piece of meat and chop into it thirty-three times. This puts any bad luck into the meat, which is then discarded. There is also a remedy for the potential problems that occur when the woman turns sixty-six. Her daughter (or closest female relative if she has no daughters), must buy some meat and cut into it sixty-six times. Again, the meat is thrown away.

For Chinese men, the dangerous year is forty. Consequently, this birthday is not celebrated, and men in China remain thirty-nine for an extra year.

All other birthdays are auspicious, and the person can look forward to a lucky day.

282. Chinese New Year

The Chinese New Year used to last for fifteen days, but nowadays it has been reduced to three days in most communities. It is a time of great celebration and family activities. The days leading up to New Year are quite busy. New clothes need to be bought, and all debts have to be repaid before the New Year starts. The house needs to be totally cleaned. This can't be done during the New Year celebrations in case the family's good luck is accidentally swept or drained away.

In the past, peach branches were used to ward away evil spirits. Some people still believe this, but today they're bought to provide good luck. If the house doesn't own a kumquat tree, one needs to be obtained in the days leading up to the New Year. The Chinese name for kumquat (*jin ju*) is a homophone of the word "gold," and consequently this tree symbolizes money coming into the house. It's extremely lucky if the peach and kumquat trees flower or bud during the New Year period, and market gardeners do their best to ensure their plants are at the right stage of development for this to occur.

The Chinese enjoy exchanging good luck at New Year. Cups of tea and sweets made of sesame seeds, melon seeds, candied fruit, and glutinous rice are offered to guests. When they take some sweets, they leave behind a few coins wrapped in red paper. Red is a lucky color in China, and these red packets are often known as *lai see*, which means "good luck piece."

Twelve

....

Folklore and Luck

Introduction

Because life is full of dangers real and imagined, folk traditions have been extremely popular as a way to attract good luck. Some of the ideas in this chapter may seem foolish to people living in the twenty-first century, but as long as people feel uncertain about their futures, they'll use these—and other similar—methods to help put luck on their side.

I have an acorn sitting on my desk. One of my granddaughters gave it to me several years ago, and I've kept it ever since as a good luck charm. I often pick up an acorn if I happen to find one while out walking. I solemnly thank it for providing me with good luck, and keep it in my pocket for a day or two. It's a small ritual that makes me feel good, and because of this I'm sure it makes me more alert for potential opportunities. I also cross my fingers, knock on wood, and do several other things in this chapter. After all, who knows? These actions might increase my luck.

Select one or two things from this section, and try them out for a few days to see what difference they make to your attitude and approach to life. A friend of mine wrote his favorite number on the back of a business card and placed it where it would be the first thing he saw each time he opened his wallet. Whenever he saw it, he felt motivated and enthusiastic. Because of this, he also felt lucky.

Another friend keeps a photograph of a chrysanthemum in her purse. It's her favorite flower, and whenever she sees it, she thinks of the pleasant hours she's spent working in her garden. This makes her realize how lucky she is.

I even put my barbecue apron on inside out during a particularly bad day. I have no idea if this gave me good luck, but the ridiculousness of it made me immediately feel happier, and the rest of the day went well.

283. Acorn

Acorns have always been considered a symbol of good luck. Because oaks are long-living trees, people felt that carrying an acorn as an amulet would enable them to both remain young at heart, and to lead a long life. An old superstition says that a house will not be struck by lightning if at least one acorn is resting on a windowsill. This belief comes from the legend that the Norse god Thor sheltered under an oak tree during a thunderstorm.

Acorns are plentiful and easy to keep in a pocket or purse. Whether you believe it will work, or not, it might be a good idea to carry one with you to ensure good luck and a long life.

284. Fingers Crossed

People around the world cross their fingers for luck when they're starting something new. I remember crossing my fingers behind my back when I was a child, because I was telling a lie and thought this would cancel out the untruth. Traditionally, people crossed their fingers while telling a lie because they believed the devil wouldn't be able to come and get them. I've met people who cross their fingers while passing graveyards for the same reason.

People frequently cross their fingers for luck when gambling or taking a minor risk.

People also cross their legs and arms to attract good luck.

285. Fishing

If you want to have good luck when you're out fishing, you should spit on your bait before casting your line. Don't be tempted to change rods when out fishing, as this creates bad luck. Of course, you can change rods if your first rod gets damaged in some way. It's important to break in a new rod in the right location. If it's a lightweight rod, for instance, you should break it in somewhere where there are plenty of the right sized fish. It's good luck to fish against the wind.

Fishermen traditionally throw back the first fish they catch in the day, which attracts good luck. And if a group of fishermen go out together, the first one to catch a fish will enjoy good luck for the rest of the day.

286. Knock on Wood

Knocking on wood, or touching wood if you're from the United Kingdom, is an ancient way of asking for good luck. In Pagan times, trees were believed to have souls to house gods. Consequently, they could be asked to protect the crops, provide rain in times of drought, and even help infertile couples to have children.

By knocking on wood, you are acknowledging and communicating with the god, or the soul of the tree, to ask for protection. Nowadays, instead of asking for good luck by knocking on wood, we ask for protection and acknowledge that luck has paid a role in our success.

287. Finding Good Luck

Traditionally, it's considered lucky to find a button, a four-leaf clover, a coin, a horseshoe, a pencil, a pin, a postage stamp, a yellow ribbon, or anything that's purple. It's important from a luck point of view to pick the item up. If you don't, the good luck will remain with the object and pass on to the first person who picks it up.

The luck of a coin is doubled if it's found heads-up.

288. Lucky Pin

It's a sign of good luck to see a pin and pick it up. As the rhyme goes, "All day long you'll have good luck." However, this doesn't apply to all pins, only ordinary straight pins and closed safety pins. If the safety pin is open when you find it, it's too late as all the luck will have vanished. Pins can be both lucky and unlucky, depending on the situation. Because they are sharp and pointed, they are potentially dangerous. Pins can protect you, but they can also harm you.

If you happen to be out somewhere and see a pin on the ground, you should pick it up as long as its point is facing away from you. This creates good luck. However, you "pick up sorrow" if you pick up a pin that is pointing toward you.

289. Housewarming

There are many good luck traditions that are invoked when moving house. You can draw good luck into the house by walking through every room while holding a loaf of a bread and a plate of salt. You can't take an old broom into your new home, as that invites bad luck. A new broom brings good luck with it. The luckiest days for moving into a new home are Monday and Wednesday.

290. Lucky Clothes

Wearing anything blue will increase your luck. This is because heaven is blue (up in the sky), and consequently negative energies are repelled by this color. Brides traditionally wear something blue to attract good luck.

291. Lucky Ring

You can make an effective lucky charm from a piece of string. Tie it into a circle to symbolize a ring, and keep it in your wallet or purse. Touch it each time you open your wallet or purse, and you'll receive good luck.

If you're not progressing as quickly as you'd like, change the rings on your fingers and folklore says you'll notice an immediate improvement in your luck.

292. Getting Dressed

When getting dressed in the morning, you should put the right sock or stocking on first. You should also put your right arm first into a shirt or blouse. These actions ensure you'll have good luck throughout the day. Folklore also says that a man who puts his right leg into his trousers first will always be the master of the house. If he puts his left foot in first, he'll be henpecked and receive little respect from other members of the household. He'll attract good luck if he puts both legs into his trousers at the same time.

It's good luck to accidentally put on an item of clothing inside out. This dates back to William the Conqueror, who accidentally put his chain mail on backwards before the Battle of Hastings. His courtiers were upset, as they considered this a bad omen. However, William reassured them by saying it was a good sign as he was about to progress from a duke to a king. It's also good luck to accidentally put on mismatched stockings or socks. However, the luck remains only if you continue to wear the item or items that way for the rest of the day.

293. New Year's Eve

There are many folk traditions performed all around the world to provide luck in the upcoming year. In Bolivia, for instance, people eat twelve grapes at midnight. In Scotland, people believe that the first person to cross the threshold of the house determines the luck of the occupants. Consequently, at midnight the perfect visitor is a dark-haired man with a coin, a lump of coal, and a small piece of bread. It's even better if he also carries a bottle of whisky. These symbolize money, food, and warmth.

A traditional belief says that anyone who finishes a bottle of alcohol on New Year's Eve will enjoy good luck in the months ahead.

Having plenty of food and drink in the cupboards on New Year's Eve symbolically demonstrates that you'll always have plenty to eat and drink in the next twelve months.

All outstanding debts should be paid on New Year's Eve. This ensures there'll be no unexpected debts in the next twelve months.

Staying up until midnight to welcome the New Year in is a popular pastime. It used to be called "ringing in" the new year, as all the church bells were rung at midnight. The custom of celebrating until the New Year arrived was originally done to drive away evil spirits. Consequently, parties were supposed to be noisy as well as joyful.

294. New Clothes on New Year's Day

Folklore says you'll receive a year of good luck if you wear new clothes on New Year's Day. Red clothes are believed to be highly auspicious, and foretell that you'll receive many more new items of clothing during the upcoming year.

295. If You're Born on January 1

January 1 is said to be the luckiest day of the year. Consequently, if you were born on this day, it's said that good luck will follow you everywhere you go. However, this doesn't protect you from stupidity and excessive risk-taking!

296. Dancing Around a Tree

Another charming superstition says you'll enjoy a year of good luck if you dance around a tree on New Year's Day. The tree must be outdoors. You can't dance around your Christmas tree, for instance.

Many years ago, I knew a lady who danced around her potted plants before bringing them indoors for winter. She believed this created good luck for both her and the plants.

297. Rubbing Your Way to Luck

Most people know that it's lucky to rub the ample stomach of the Laughing Buddha. They may not realize that the Laughing Buddha is actually Budai, an eccentric monk who lived in China eleven hundred years ago.

It's also common to rub the head of a bald man for luck. One baldheaded man I know dislikes this but puts up with it as he says he's bound to receive a bit of good luck for allowing the rubbing to happen. Other friends say they like it, as it gives them special attention and gives them good luck. Justin Verlander, the Detroit Tigers pitcher, was recorded rubbing the head of Doug Teter, the team's trainer, for luck.[1]

Rubbing the statue of a famous person also provides good luck. The nose and the feet are supposed to be the luckiest places to rub.

The word *rub* has another meaning, too. People enjoy sitting next to lucky people as they hope some of the good luck will rub off onto them.

298. Catch a Falling Leaf

People all around the world believe that catching a leaf as it falls from a tree attracts good luck. You need to keep the leaf in a safe place to ensure the good luck continues to flow your way.

299. Catch a Falling Star

It's a sign of extreme good luck if two lovers happen to see a falling star at the same time. They should make a wish as soon as they see it. Falling stars are also lucky for travelers, people who are unwell, and people who are searching for a partner.

Perry Como's famous song "Catch a Falling Star," written by Paul Vance and Lee Pockriss, was recorded in 1957. It's remained popular for many reasons, including its positive, upbeat message.

300. Keep a Penny in Your Shoes

Keeping a penny in one of your shoes is said to be a good way to attract good luck, especially if the coin was minted in the year you were born.

301. Silver Coins and the New Moon

You can attract good luck by placing two or more silver coins in the palm of your left hand on the night of the new moon. Go outside and gaze at the moon while gently rubbing the coins with the fingers of your right hand.

302. Caterpillar

Hairy caterpillars are considered a sign of good luck. To activate the luck, you need to pick the caterpillar up and toss it over your shoulder. This might not be lucky for the caterpillar, but is said to be good for the person who finds it.

303. From Left to Right

Sir Winston Churchill loved champagne, and at the start of any important meal a bottle of chilled champagne would be placed in front of him. Churchill would pour a glass for himself, and everyone else within reach. After this, he would pass the bottle to his left and tell the other guests to help themselves.

It was important for Churchill to pass the glass to his left. He was acting on an old superstition that says it's good luck to pass to the left. (Conversely, it's bad luck to pass to the right.) It's good luck because in the northern hemisphere the sun appears to cross the sky from left to right if you're facing south.

304. Pricking a Finger

If you accidentally prick your finger on your birthday, you should allow three drops of blood to fall onto a clean handkerchief. If you carry this handkerchief with you, it will bring you good luck.

305. Lucky Rainbows

Seeing a rainbow is a sign of good luck, as it symbolizes the bridging of the natural and supernatural worlds. In the United Kingdom, it's lucky to see a rainbow as long as you don't point at it. Pointing at a rainbow brings instant bad luck.

There's a charming story told in many parts of the world saying that there's a pot of gold at the end of the rainbow. Even if there's no pot of gold, the spot where the rainbow touches the ground is said to be lucky. The legend of the pot of gold at the end of the rainbow relates to how the sight of a rainbow can bring positivity and good luck. It's considered especially good luck to see both ends of the rainbow. Many people make a wish whenever they see a rainbow.

In Norse legend, a rainbow is said to be a bridge for souls that leads to the land of the gods. In parts of Europe, the souls of deceased children are said to travel along a rainbow to get to heaven. Their guardian angels keep them company along the way.

In the Bible, God created a rainbow as a token of the covenant made with Noah that he would never again destroy the world with a flood. "And God said, 'This is the token of the covenant which I make between me and you and every living creature that is with you, for perpetual generations: I do set my bow in the cloud, and it shall be for a covenant between me and the earth'" (Genesis 9:12–13). As Noah saw a rainbow near the end of his time on the ark, some people believe that a rainbow is a sign that God will never flood the entire world again.

In 1978, Gilbert Baker created a rainbow flag for the San Francisco Gay and Lesbian Freedom Day Parade. It quickly became the international symbol of gay pride, and in 1986 was recognized by the International Flag Association as a genuine flag.

306. Sneezing

Most people are not aware that sneezing twice is a sign of good luck. Sneezing once or three times is bad luck. In the past, many people believed that the soul could escape from the body during a sneeze. Saying, "God bless you" or "Gesundheit" ("good health") protected the person until his or her soul returned again. Saying these words also provides good luck to you and the person who is sneezing.

It's also a sign of good luck for a sick person to sneeze. This is said to be a sign that he or she is recovering. The first sneeze a baby makes is also a sign of good luck. This is because people used to believe that people with low intelligence couldn't sneeze. Consequently, parents would be highly relieved when their baby sneezed for the first time.

It's a sign of good luck for the whole family when their cat sneezes. It's also good luck if two people happen to sneeze at the same time.

307. Specks on the Fingernails

White spots on the fingernails are a sign of good luck, and an indication that money is on its way. An old English rhyme refers to this:

Specks on the fingers,
Fortune lingers.
Specks on the thumb,
Fortune surely comes.

The first reference to lucky spots on fingernails can be found in *The Zohar* (ii. 76a), a Jewish mystical text that was first published in the thirteenth century, but is said to be hundreds of years older than that.

308. Lucky Numbers

Certain numbers have always been considered lucky. The ancient art of numerology, which describes character and predicts the future using numbers from people's dates of birth, meant people were familiar with the concept of lucky and unlucky numbers.

If the sum of all the numbers in your date of birth is divisible by seven, you will be protected and lucky throughout life.

If someone asks you to name your lucky number, the chances are you'll say an odd number. Odd numbers, with the exception of thirteen, are considered luckier than even numbers. More than two thousand years ago, Virgil (70–19 BCE) wrote in his eighth *Eclogue*: "God delights in odd numbers." Chinese pagodas always contain an odd number of stories. They provide good luck to the area they are built in.

Most lucky numbers are single digits. However, a few people pick eleven and twenty-two, as these are called "master numbers" in numerology.

309. One

One is a lucky number as it is associated with one God and one sun. It is associated with creation and life itself. People born on the first of any month are said to be luckier than people born on other days.

310. Two

Two is a lucky number as it symbolizes harmony, balance, and the two sexes. As two is comprised of two ones, this number is associated with pairs, such as man and woman, and love and marriage. Number one relates to the sun, and two relates to the moon.

311. Three

Three is considered a lucky number. Pythagoras (c.580–c.500), the Greek philosopher and mathematician, considered three to be the perfect number. The Greek prophetess Pythia sat on a three-legged stool to make her prognostications. Three symbolizes the miracle of birth, as a man and a woman create a child. Three also symbolizes birth, life, and death. In Christianity, three is the number of the Trinity. In China, the third day of the new moon is considered the luckiest of the month. The triangle has three sides, and is considered a potent magical symbol that wards off evil. Many lucky rituals need to be repeated three times. There is also a strong belief that the third attempt at anything is "a charm." We also have three cheers, three wishes, and three strikes before you're out.

312. Four

Four is considered the luckiest even number, as so many important things come in fours. For instance, there are four cardinal directions, four gospels, four evangelists, and four suits in decks of tarot and regular playing cards. There are also the four classical elements of fire, earth, air, and water. There are four seasons: spring, summer, autumn or fall, and winter. There are also four qualities: hot, cold, moist, and dry.

313. Five

Five was possibly considered lucky as people have five fingers on each hand and five toes on each foot. The ancient Greeks and Romans considered five to be a lucky number, and used a five-pointed star as a protective amulet. In Roman weddings, guests were introduced in groups of five. Five wise and five foolish virgins are mentioned in the Bible. There are also five elements in Eastern philosophy: fire, earth, water, metal, and wood.

314. Six

Six symbolizes creation, as God created the world in six days and rested on the seventh. Six is considered a perfect number as it is the sum of $1+2+3$. People born on the sixth of the month are believed to have a talent at foretelling the future. Six is an unlucky number for dishonest people.

315. Seven

The ancient Greeks considered seven to be the perfect number. This was because it is the sum of the triangle and square, which are considered perfect shapes. They also noticed the phases of the moon that change every seven days. There are seven days in a week, seven deadly sins, and seven wonders of the ancient world. In the Bible, God created the world in six days and rested on the seventh. Five planets, plus the sun and moon, can be seen by the human eye, and there are seven colors in a rainbow. Seven cannot be divided by any other number. The seventh son of a seventh son is believed to have the gift of second sight, as well as healing powers. There are seven gods of luck in Japanese folklore. The Islamic seventh heaven is the home of God and people say they're in "seventh heaven" when they're overjoyed and full of happiness.

It's said to be good luck to have seven letters in your first or last name. Seven is supposed to be a particularly lucky number for gamblers.

316. Eight

The ancient Pythagoreans considered eight a solid, reliable number. Eight was a symbol of the Egyptian god Thoth, who poured the water of purification on the heads of people initiated to his religion. Emanuel Swedenborg (1688–1772), the Swedish mystic, also related eight to purification. Eight is considered a lucky number for people seeking financial and material success.

Eight has always been considered a lucky number in China as it is a sign of money in the near future. 888 is an extremely fortunate number in China as it means "wealth, wealth, wealth."

317. Nine

Nine is considered a lucky number as it is the sum of three, a lucky number, multiplied by itself. As the period from conception to birth is nine months, nine is often associated with fertility. A number of expressions use the number nine. A cat has nine lives, someone can become a nine-day wonder, and a stitch in time can save nine.

318. Ten

Ten has been considered a lucky number for thousands of years. As human beings have ten fingers and ten toes, it has always symbolized completion. Aristotle considered ten to be "the total of all things." The Pythagoreans considered ten to symbolize all of creation, and depicted it as a star with ten points. In the Jewish tradition, it is the number of completion, which might explain why God revealed ten commandments to Moses. In China, ten symbolizes balance.

319. Eleven

Eleven is considered a lucky number as, according to numerology, it enables the person who chooses it to develop psychically and spiritually, until he or she is able to inspire others with his or her example.

320. Twelve

Twelve symbolized space and time in ancient astronomy and astrology. This is why we have twelve signs of the zodiac, twelve months in the year, and twelve hours each of day- and nighttime. The Chinese have twelve groups of years in their system of astrology. In the later Greek tradition, twelve gods ruled Mount Olympus. Twelve plays an important role in the Judeo-Christian tradition. Jacob had twelve sons, and consequently the twelve tribes of Israel. There were twelve jewels in the priest's breastplate. Jesus had twelve disciples. Christians celebrate the twelve days of Christmas.

Twelve is considered a lucky number in any dealings involving time, such as twelve hours, days, weeks, months, or years.

321. Thirteen

It's fascinating how things change over time. Nowadays, thirteen is considered an unlucky number, but in the past it meant the opposite. There's a tradition that says anyone born on Friday the thirteenth of any month will always be lucky.

In Judaism, boys celebrate their bar mitzah when they're thirteen. In addition, the Orthodox Jewish prayer book includes "the thirteen principles of faith" and discusses the thirteen attributes of God.

There are thirteen stripes on the flag of the United States. These symbolize the thirteen original colonies. The Great Seal of the United States is on the back of the one dollar bill. It contains several thirteens in it. The eagle's shield contains thirteen stripes, the eagle's left talon holds thirteen arrows, and the right talon holds an olive branch with thirteen leaves and thirteen berries. The circle above the eagle's head contains a constellation of thirteen stars. Even the Latin motto in the eagle's beak (*E Pluribus Unum*) contains thirteen letters. The reverse side of the Great Seal is also shown on the reverse side of the bill. It contains a pyramid built from thirteen layers of stone. The Latin phrase above the pyramid (*Annuit Coeptis*) also contains thirteen letters. All these thirteens relate to the original thirteen colonies, and symbolize regeneration, renewal, and a new world.

Gamblers, who are amongst the most superstitious people of all, consider thirteen a lucky number. "Lucky" thirteen is a popular number to play, especially on Friday the thirteenth.

322. Twenty-Two

Twenty-two is sometimes referred to as the "master builder" in numerology. It's a lucky number, as it gives the person who chooses it the potential to develop enormous power that can benefit all humanity. Unfortunately, it usually remains as a potential, as it is extremely difficult to harness and use the energies provided by this number.

323. Pea Pods

Most people buy their peas, rather than growing them, and consequently miss out on a charming way of gaining good luck. If you're shelling peas and happen to find a single pea in a pod, you'll be lucky for a whole month. If you find nine peas in a pod, the luck will last for twelve months. This luck is doubled if you find one or nine peas in the very first pod you shell.

324. Wishbone

If you're fortunate enough to receive the wishbone while eating chicken, you can make a wish with it. You may do this immediately by crooking your little finger around one end of the wishbone and offering the other end to the person next to you. Once he or she has a little finger crooked around the other end, you can pull together while making a silent wish. The person who receives the larger part of the bone will have his or her wish granted.

Alternatively, you can put the wishbone to one side and allow it to dry out thoroughly, and then go through the same procedure.

It's important that you take this opportunity seriously. Consequently, you shouldn't laugh or make jokes while holding a wishbone. You must keep your wish a secret until after it has been granted.

The furcula, better known as the wishbone, from a chicken or turkey makes an extremely potent good luck charm. When the wishbone is pulled, both people need to make a wish. The person who receives the capped end will have his or her wish granted. Less well known is that the other person will also receive some good luck in the near future.

The origin of this belief is unknown, but it probably relates to the crowing of the rooster to announce the coming day, and the clucking of a hen to indicate she'll shortly be laying an egg. This showed they were able to see into the future.

325. Carnation

The carnation is considered a lucky flower for people born in January. It is considered a symbol of female love. An old legend says the carnation first appeared on earth to celebrate the birth of Christ. It's a nice story, but there is evidence that the carnation was present well before the birth of Jesus. A superstition about carnations says that the plant grew beside the graves of lovers. Because of this, it became popular as a flower in funeral wreaths. On a brighter note, carnations are also said to restore the joys of life to people suffering from melancholy.

326. Violet

The violet is considered a lucky flower for people born in February. The ancient Greeks had several legends about the origin of this flower. One day Orpheus placed his lyre on the ground. When he picked it up again he discovered violets growing under it. Napoleon Bonaparte loved violets and wore one as his badge of honor when he was exiled. Because of this, he was frequently called "Corporal Violette," and violets were banned in France for many years after the Battle of Waterloo.

327. Daffodil

The daffodil is considered a lucky flower for people born in March. In the nineteenth century, Wales adopted the daffodil as a symbol. William Wordsworth wrote his famous poem *Daffodils* after being inspired by the beauty of its flowers. If the narcissus flowers during the Chinese New Year, it's a sign of good luck, wealth, and abundance.

An old tradition says that the first person in the household to see a daffodil at the start of spring will receive good luck during the next twelve months. It's good luck to bring bunches of daffodils indoors, but it's considered bad luck to bring a single daffodil inside on its own.

328. Daisy

The daisy is considered a lucky flower for people born in April. In folklore it's related to innocence, purity, and peace of mind. An old tradition says that if a newly married woman wants a child, she should keep a daisy inside her left stocking. Even today children pull the petals of a daisy while reciting, "s/he love me, s/he loves me not" to see if someone truly loves them. Even though it's a common, often overlooked flower, it's a sign of true love to give one to the special person in your life. The daisy is a lucky flower for people in love.

329. Lily of the Valley

Lily of the valley is considered a lucky flower for people born in May. An old legend says that these flowers were created by Eve's tears as she left the Garden of Eden. In Ireland, they say lily of the valley is a small ladder. Fairies are said to run up and down this ladder ringing bells.

Christians dedicated the lily of the valley to the Virgin Mary, which is why it is a symbol of purity. In the United Kingdom, this plant is still sometimes called "our Lady's tears."

As well as attracting good luck, this flower is also said to be able to cheer up even the saddest person.

330. Honeysuckle

The honeysuckle is considered a lucky flower for people born in June. The Chinese use it as a powerful herb that eliminates toxins from the body. In much of Asia, the honeysuckle symbolizes longevity because its winding vines join together and appear to have no end. In Europe, the honeysuckle symbolizes love and protection, and it's good luck to grow it in your garden. If you display the flowers indoors they will attract prosperity.

331. Water Lily

The water lily is considered a lucky flower for people born in July. "Lucky bamboo," a variety of water lily, has become popular in the West, as it is said to bring luck and good fortune into the home.

332. Gladiolus

The gladiolus is considered a lucky flower for people born in August. Gardeners love this perennial plant, as it's easy to grow, and provides a profusion of beautiful flowers. They are thought to be the plants that Jesus called "lilies of the field" because they are so abundant in the Holy Land. They help people gain strength of character, and they also help people who are looking for a partner.

333. Morning Glory

The morning glory is considered a lucky flower for people born in September. In folk magic it's used to provide confidence, strength, success, and good luck. The root of this plant is called John the Conqueror in Hoodoo, and it is rubbed to provide good luck in gambling and love.

334. Calendula

The calendula is considered a lucky flower for people born in October. It is also considered a lucky herb for anyone involved in money matters, especially gambling. Gamblers would put some calendula petals into a small bag, which they placed under their pillow. This encouraged prophetic dreams that included lucky numbers. Wreaths of calendula leaves used to be hung over doors to prevent evil spirits from entering the home. The smell of calendula helps people realize that they already possess all the talents they need to make a success of this incarnation.

335. Chrysanthemum

The chrysanthemum is considered a lucky flower for people born in November. It was a popular flower in ancient Egypt and Greece, and has always been popular in Japan and China. The chrysanthemum symbolizes perfection to the Japanese, and the Supreme Order of the Chrysanthemum is the highest possible honor one can receive in Japan. In China, the chrysanthemum is a symbol of longevity and perfection. Drinking water with chrysanthemums was considered lucky, and people believed it would enable people to live longer, and enjoy a life of ease. Chrysanthemum petals are popular as garnish for salads.

336. Narcissus

Narcissus is the botanical name for daffodil, and is considered a lucky flower for people born in December. However, because of the legend about a young man called Narcissus, this plant has been associated with egotism and self-love for thousands of years. Narcissus loved only himself. One day he was admiring his reflection in a pool of water and fell in while trying to touch it. When his body was recovered, it had changed into a flower. Despite this sad story, the narcissus is lucky for anyone born in December, and anyone seeking worthwhile goals.

337. Holly

In ancient Rome, holly symbolized friendship, and was given to friends in midwinter as a gesture of goodwill. In northern Europe, people hung holly on their doors to create good luck. They also believed wood spirits sheltered from the cold winds inside holly plants, and would provide protection for the home.

Holly became associated with Christianity as people thought the crown of thorns that Jesus wore was made of holly. They also believed the holly's berries were originally yellow, but became red after the Crucifixion to symbolize Christ's blood.

In addition to being a charming Christmas symbol, holly provides protection for the home and attracts good luck and happiness to the people who live there.

338. Myrtle

The Greeks dedicated the myrtle to Aphrodite and considered it a symbol of love. In Rome, groves of myrtle surrounded the temple of Venus. The association with love still applies in Wales. Couples plant myrtle on each side of their home to preserve their love and to ensure harmony in the home. Myrtle is considered a sign of good luck in the United Kingdom.

339. Beginner's Luck

An old superstition says that beginners in any field of activity receive a special sort of luck. This may or may not be true; however, the law of averages ensures that any special luck beginners might possess is only temporary. In English football, it's traditional for the oldest person on the team to pass the ball to the newest member as the final part of the warm-up before a game. This ensures that the beginner's luck will extend to every member of the team.

340. Breath

Breath has always been associated with the spirit, and many ancient words for "breath" also meant "spirit." The Hebrew *ruach*, Greek *pneuma*, and Latin *spiritus* are all examples. The concept of breathing on something for luck is thousands of years old, and is still practiced today. Gamblers frequently blow on their cards or dice for luck, and people who buy lottery tickets blow on them for the same reason.

341. Wishing Well

People have made wishes while tossing coins into ponds, springs, wells, and fountains for thousands of years. This came about because water is essential for all life. Consequently, anywhere water appeared to come from was considered holy, and people believed it was looked after by spirits and gods. Prayers and sacrifices were made to these spirits to encourage prosperity and good luck.

Today it's considered a charming tradition, but the ritual of formulating a wish and tossing a coin helps people focus on a specific desire and consequently attracts good luck.

342. Double Your Luck

I learned this tradition on a recent visit to the United Kingdom. I was walking along a village street with two good friends and happened to notice a ten pence coin lying on the road. I bent down to pick it up, and as soon as I stood up again, my friend handed me another coin and said, "Double your luck!" Apparently, your luck is doubled if someone immediately hands you a coin of the same denomination as the one you've found. I bought a tiny bag to keep them in, and whenever I become aware of it in my pocket I say to myself, "Double your luck!"

343. Playing Cards

An old saying says that people who are lucky with cards are unlucky in love, and vice versa. If the game of cards is not going your way, you can change your luck by blowing on the cards while shuffling them.

If you have a lucky card, you should touch it with your index finger before starting to play.

344. Chimney Sweep

Hundreds of years before Julie Andrews sang about luck and chimney sweeps in *Mary Poppins*, chimney sweeps were considered to carry good luck with them everywhere they went. This tradition began in eighteenth-century England when a sweep saved a king on a runaway horse. Before the king had time to thank him, the sweep had disappeared into the crowd. Some sources say it was King George III who was saved by the chimney sweep.

Kissing or shaking hands with a chimney sweep is extremely lucky, and ensures a happy marriage. It's good luck for a bride to see a chimney sweep while on the way to her wedding. In the United Kingdom, it's possible to hire a chimney sweep to be at the right place at the right time to ensure that the bride-to-be sees him as she goes past.

345. Lucky Circle

The circle has always been a symbol of completeness, wholeness, perfection, and good luck. It probably gained the good luck association because of the sun's apparent circle around the earth.

Because the circle was lucky, people started thinking that evil spirits would not be able to cross it. Consequently, wreaths, rings, and other circular items were invented to provide protection. Even lipstick became associated with this. Because people thought evil spirits could enter the body through the mouth, they started painting a red circle around it to provide protection.

346. Lucky Feather

It's a sign of good luck to find a feather. You should pick it up and stick it into the ground. The luck is doubled if you find a black feather. Many people believe white feathers come from angels, and they're a sign of protection and good luck. If you find a white feather, you might decide to keep it as a good luck charm.

347. Iron

Iron has been considered lucky since prehistoric times. People watched meteors flying through space and landing on the earth. As the metal must have come from heaven, weapons made from this meteoric iron must have seemed like a special gift from the gods. People armed with weapons made from iron could easily defeat people without metal weapons. This increased the belief in the powerful, magical, and lucky properties of iron.

Even today, some people place an iron object such as a knife under a doormat to protect the home and provide good luck.

348. Leaves

It's considered good luck for dead leaves to blow into your home. However, it's considered bad luck to carry dead leaves inside.

It's also good luck to catch leaves as they fall from a tree. You need to catch them before they touch the ground. Each leaf caught provides a month of good luck.

349. Orange

The orange is considered a lucky fruit, especially for lovers. Folklore says that if a young man gives his girlfriend an orange their love will grow.

Orange blossom is a well-known floral fertility symbol that was introduced into Europe by soldiers returning from the Crusades. The tradition of decorating a bride with orange blossoms began in France and was introduced to England in the early nineteenth century. The white blossom is a symbol of innocence, and the fruit signifies fruitfulness. Consequently, brides carry orange blossoms for luck and to ensure the marriage will produce children.

350. Sage

Sage is considered a lucky plant for many reasons. It is said to improve the memory, provide wisdom, avert the evil eye, ease the pain of childbirth, absorb negativity, and provide good luck. Surprisingly, with all of these things in its favor, it's considered unlucky to plant it in your own garden! It's best to obtain your sage from someone else.

You can also write a wish on a sage leaf and then burn it to send the wish out into the universe. As long as you believe it will work, your wish will be granted.

351. Baker's Dozen

The term "baker's dozen" means thirteen items, rather than twelve. The expression dates back at least five hundred years, and its origin is unknown. It probably came about when bakers included an extra loaf with every twelve to protect them from being accused of short-weighing the loaves. I remember my mother always being delighted when our local baker gave us a baker's dozen when she bought bread rolls or buns. She considered it good luck.

When we buy coffee beans at our local coffee shop, the owner weighs them carefully, and then deliberately adds a little bit more. He calls this his "baker's dozen." Nowadays, it seems to mean receiving a little bit more than expected. Whenever this happens to you, remind yourself how lucky you are.

352. Shoelaces

It's a sign of good luck to find that your shoelaces have formed a knot. It means good luck will stay with you all day. You can make a silent wish for yourself while doing up someone else's shoelaces. It's bad luck to wear shoelaces of different colors. Brown and black is a particularly bad combination, as black is the color of death, and brown is the color of the earth in the graveyard.

353. Shoes

The tradition of tying an old boot to the back of the bridal car came about because shoes are considered lucky. You can increase your luck by standing on the toes of a new pair of shoes. Children often do this for fun, not knowing that it was originally done to create good luck.

354. Silver

Silver has always been considered a lucky metal, and people often collect items made from it for both aesthetic purposes and to ensure their future prosperity. Silver coins and antique silver are examples of silver objects that are sought after by collectors and investors who often have no idea that they're also increasing their luck at the same time.

355. Thimble

People seldom make their own clothes nowadays, but some traditions applicable to this still apply. Thimbles, for instance, are still given for luck. However, it's bad luck to be given three of them at the same time, as this means the recipient will never marry. My grandmother made wedding gowns, and had a huge collection of thimbles she'd been given by her clients. She kept them on display in the room she worked in to attract good luck.

It's good luck for the owner of a garment if a seamstress loses a thimble while working on it. However, this doesn't apply if she is working on her own garment.

356. Under a Full Moon

A child who is born under a full moon will be healthy, strong, and enjoy good luck throughout life. Girls born under the full moon will be beautiful and graceful. It's also lucky to get married under a full moon, or up to two days before or after the full moon. This is said to ensure good luck and prosperity. It's good luck to have a full moon on the moon's day (Monday).

357. Lucky Dreams

It's good luck to wake up knowing that you've been dreaming, but to be unable to remember it. This means the dream was important, and the lesson it gave you will have been accepted by your subconscious mind.

If you remember your dreams, you should not tell anyone about them until after you've eaten breakfast.

358. Shaking Hands

When two people shake hands after making a deal, they are expressing their good intentions to each other and to the deal. They are also symbolically wishing it luck. This is because the two hands form the sign of the cross, which is considered a sign of good luck.

359. Bloom Where You're Planted

One of the best stand-up comedians I've ever seen lives in a small town, and won't accept work that is more than four hours drive from his home. When I asked him why he didn't expand his horizons, he said, "I choose to bloom where I was planted." I hadn't heard the expression before, and he explained that it relates to the fact that many people believe they'd be luckier if they lived somewhere else.

"There's no guarantee I'd be successful if I went to New York or L.A.," he told me. "I'd have to leave my family and friends behind. They're a big part of my life. I'm happy and do well here. You could say I'm a big fish in a small pond. Why would I uproot myself when I don't need to?"

There's no guarantee that your luck would be different in another town or country. If you're happy living where you are, there's no need to move anywhere else. Seize the opportunities you find, work hard, and create your own luck.

360. Cake

Traditionally, wedding cakes were made to bring good luck to the bride and groom, and all the wedding guests too. An old tradition says cake should be eaten at any celebration—such as a birthday—or at the start of anything new to provide good luck to everyone involved.

At one time, cake charms were made to provide protection for individuals and families. A sheet of paper containing texts from the Gospel of

St. John were baked inside the cake. These cakes were not eaten, but kept to provide protection and good luck.[2]

361. Apron

In the past, an apron was an almost essential part of many women's clothing. It was considered good luck to accidentally put on an apron inside out. In fact, if you were having a frustrating day, you could improve your luck by deliberately putting an apron on inside out.

362. Dice

All around the world people gamble and play games with dice. Because they're often used in games of chance such as crapshooting, they've become one of the most popular symbols of good luck. A friend of mine who is a keen gambler carries a pair of dice everywhere with him, as he believes he'll be lucky and never run out of money as long as they're in his possession.

363. Speech

You are likely to have experienced the situation where you said something at the exact moment that someone else said the same words. This is considered extremely lucky for both people, according to folklore. In fact, it's so lucky that the two people should each make a silent wish before speaking again.

364. Hug a Tree

Many people hug trees to feel grounded and to reconnect with the energy of the planet. Other people hug trees to attract good luck. If you decide to try this, choose a tree that appeals to you aesthetically. There is no right or wrong way to hug a tree. You can wrap your arms around its trunk, lean against it, sit with your back in contact with the tree, or simply stroke it. You'll feel calmer and more relaxed after hugging a tree and this change in outlook will increase your chances of gaining good luck.

365. Lucks

"Lucks" are family heirlooms that have been passed down from generation to generation. They are said to bring good luck to whomever is looking after them. Lucks are normally small objects such as cups, spoons, dishes, or ornaments that were originally given to one of your ancestors. To make the best use of one, thank it regularly for increasing the luck of your family. Look after it, and if appropriate, display it somewhere in your home where you'll see it regularly.

One of the best known examples is displayed in the Victoria and Albert Museum in London. This is the Edenhall Cup, which was owned by the Musgrove family of Cumberland from the fifteenth century until it was acquired by the British government in 1958. The Edenhall Cup of gilded and enamelled glass was made in Egypt or Syria in the fourteenth century.[3] In 1721, the Duke of Wharton almost ended the family's luck by accidentally dropping it. Fortunately, the butler caught it before it hit the ground.

Thirteen

....

Conclusion

Throughout history, everyone from kings to beggars has tried to entice good luck. Yet, despite extensive research, luck remains elusive and hard to pin down. In fact, we know little more about the subject than the ancient Egyptians, Greeks, and Romans did thousands of years ago.

Luck explains how one person receives a series of lucky opportunities while someone else with equal ability does not. The success of one and the failure of the other are both caused by luck. Luck is fickle too, and comes and goes without apparent cause. Someone can be lucky one day, and unlucky the next.

Many people throughout history have worn good luck charms. President Theodore Roosevelt had a lucky rabbit's foot, and Emperor Napoleon carried a lucky coin. President Barack Obama has several good luck charms.[1] There are good reasons to carry them, too. A 2003 university study in the United Kingdom demonstrated that people who carry lucky charms not only feel luckier, but actually become luckier.[2] This is because the lucky charm gives them confidence, and consequently increases their chances of success.

Dr. Lysann Damisch of the University of Cologne asked twenty-eight students to participate in an experiment. They were all told to bring a lucky charm with them. The charms were taken away to be photographed, but only half were returned. The students were told there was a problem with the photography and their charms would be returned later. The students were then asked to participate in a memory test involving matching cards on a computer. The students who had their lucky charm with them performed better than the other students.[3] This shows that people believe in their lucky charms, and it is this that makes them work.

Niels Bohr (1885–1962), the Danish physicist and Nobel Prize winner, had a different opinion. A visitor noticed Bohr had a horseshoe hanging over the front door of his house and asked if he believed it brought him good luck. Bohr is reputed to have replied: "Of course not. But I am told it works even if you don't believe in it."[4]

If you don't feel lucky, act as if you are. Developing and maintaining a positive mindset will help you attract all the good things life has to offer.

I hope you try out some of the ideas in this book and make up your own mind. Good luck!

Suggested Reading

The Holy Bible, King James Version. Nashville, TN: Thomas Nelson Publishers, 1984.

Aaronson, Deborah, and Kevin Kwan. *Luck: The Essential Guide*. New York: HarperCollins, 2008.

Aczel, Amir D. *Chance: A Guide to Gambling, Love, the Stock Market & Just About Everything Else*. London: High Stakes, 2005.

Alford, Henry. *How to Live: A Search for Wisdom from Old People (While They Are Still on This Earth)*. New York: Hachette Book Group, 2009.

Andrews, Carol. *Amulets of Ancient Egypt*. London: British Museum Press, 1994.

Bach, Marcus. *The World of Serendipity*. Marina Del Rey, CA: DeVorss & Company, 1970.

Banks, Syd. *The Enlightened Gardener*. Renton, WA: International Human Relations Consultants, 2001.

———. *The Enlightened Gardener Revisited*. Edmonton, Canada: Lone Pine Publishing, 2005.

Bechtel, Stefan, and Laurence Roy Stains. *The Good Luck Book*. New York: Workman Publishing, 1997.

Begley, Sharon. *Train Your Mind, Change Your Brain: How a New Science Reveals Our Extraordinary Potential to Transform Ourselves*. New York: Ballantine Books, 2007.

Carr, A. H. Z. *How to Attract Good Luck and Make the Most of It in Your Daily Life*. New York: Simon & Schuster, Inc., 1952.

Carus, Paul. *Chinese Thought: An Exposition of the Main Characteristic Features of the Chinese World-Conception*. First published 1907. Accessed May 2014: www.scribd.com/doc/107119743/Carus -Paul-Chinese-thought-An-exposition-of-the-main-characteristic -features-of-the-Chinese-world-conception-1907.

Cheung, Theresa. *Get Lucky! Make Your Own Opportunities*. Dublin, Ireland: Gill & Macmillan Ltd., 2003.

Chopra, Deepak. *The Spontaneous Fulfillment of Desire: Harnessing the Infinite Power of Coincidence*. New York: Harmony Books, 2003.

Conwell, Russell H. *Acres of Diamonds*. Philadelphia: John Y. Huber Company, 1890.

Cousins, Norman. *Anatomy of an Illness as Perceived by the Patient*. New York: W. W. Norton, Inc., 1979.

Emmons, Robert A. *The Psychology of Gratitude*. New York: Oxford University Press, 2004.

———. *Thanks! How the New Science of Gratitude Can Make You Happier*. New York: Houghton-Mifflin Company, 2007.

Fukami, Seizan. *Make Your Own Luck*. Tokyo, Japan: Tachibana Shuppan, Inc, 1994.

Gittelson, Bernard. *How to Make Your Own Luck*. New York: Warner Books, Inc., 1981.

Gunther, Max. *The Very, Very Rich and How They Got That Way*. Chicago: Playboy Press, 1972.

———. *Instant Millionaires: The Secrets of Overnight Success*. Petersfield, UK: Harriman House Ltd., 2011. Originally published by Chicago: Playboy Press, 1973.

———. *The Luck Factor: Why Some People are Luckier than Others and How You Can Become One of Them*. Petersfield, UK: Harriman House Ltd., 2009. Originally published by New York: Macmillan and Company, 1977.

———. *How to Get Lucky: 13 Techniques for Discovering and Taking Advantage of Life's Good Breaks*. Petersfield, UK: Harriman House Ltd., 2010. Originally published by New York: Stein and Day, 1986.

Hutson, Matthew. *The 7 Laws of Magical Thinking: How Irrational Beliefs Keep Us Happy, Healthy, and Sane*. New York: Hudson Street Press, 2012.

Keoghan, Phil, with Warren Berger. *No Opportunity Wasted*. Emmaus, PA: Rodale, Inc, 2004.

Kunz, George Frederick. *The Curious Lore of Precious Stones*. Philadelphia: J. B. Lippincott Company, 1913.

Levine, Leslie. *Wish It, Dream It, Do It: Turn the Life You're Living into the Life You Want*. New York: Simon & Schuster, Inc., 2004.

Llopis, Glenn. *Earning Serendipity: 4 Skills for Creating and Sustaining Good Fortune in Your Work*. Austin, TX: Greenleaf Book Group Press, 2009.

Maxey, Cyndi and Jill Bremer. *It's Your Move: Dealing Yourself the Best Cards in Life and Work*. Upper Saddle River, NJ: Prentice Hall, 2004.

Neill, Michael. *The Inside Out Revolution*. Carlsbad, CA: Hay House, 2013.

Paine, Sheila. *Amulets: A World of Secret Powers, Charms and Magic*. London: Thames & Hudson Ltd., 2004.

Pais, Abraham. *Inward Bound: Of Matters and Forces in the Physical World*. New York: Oxford University Press, 1986.

Park, Layton. *Get Out of Your Own Way: Unlocking the Power of Your Mind to Get What You Want*. Woodbury, MN: Llewellyn Publications, 2007.

Piven, Joshua. *As Luck Would Have It: Incredible Stories from Lottery Wins to Lightning Strikes*. New York: Villard Books, 2003.

Radford, E. & M. A., edited and revised by Christina Hole. *Encyclopaedia of Superstitions*. London: Hutchinson & Company, 1961.

Rescher, Nicholas. *Luck: The Brilliant Randomness of Everyday Life*. New York: Farrar Strauss Giroux, 1995.

Richards, Steve. *Luck, Chance & Coincidence: The Mysterious Power of Luck—and How to Make Yours Better*. Wellingborough, UK: The Aquarian Press, 1985.

RoAne, Susan. *How to Create Your Own Luck*. Hoboken, NJ: John Wiley & Sons, Inc., 2004.

Roberts, Royston M. *Serendipity: Accidental Discoveries in Science*. New York: John Wiley & Sons, Inc., 1989.

Robinson, Ken, with Lou Aronica. *The Element: How Finding Your Passion Changes Everything*. New York: Viking Penguin, 2009.

Seligman, Martin E. P. *Authentic Happiness: Using the New Positive Psychology to Realize Your Potential for Lasting Fulfillment*. New York: Free Press, 2002.

——. *Flourish: A Visionary New Understanding of Happiness and Well-Being*. New York: Free Press, 2011.

Shapiro, Eileen C., and Howard H. Stevenson. *Make Your Own Luck: 12 Practical Steps to Taking Smarter Risks in Business*. New York: Penguin, 2005.

Shenk, David. *The Genius in All of Us: Why Everything You've Been Told About Genetics, Talent, and IQ is Wrong*. New York: Doubleday, 2010.

Smith, Daniel. *The Lucky Bugger's Casebook: Tales of Serendipity and Outrageous Good Fortune*. London: Icon Books Limited, 2009.

Smith, Ed. *Luck: What it Means and Why It Matters*. London: Bloomsbury Books, 2012.

Summers, Heather, and Anne Watson. *The Book of Luck: Brilliant Ideas for Creating Your Own Success and Making Life Go Your Way*. Chichester, UK: Capstone Publishing, 2005.

Vinci, Leo. *Talismans, Amulets and Charms*. London: Regency Press, 1977.

Wallis Budge, E. A. *Amulets and Superstitions*. London: Oxford University Press, 1930.

Weaver, Warren. *Lady Luck: The Theory of Probability*. London: Heinemann Educational Books, 1964.

Weber, Max., trans. A. M. Henderson and Talcott Parsons. *The Theory of Social and Economic Organization*. New York: Oxford University Press, 1947.

Webster, Richard. *101 Feng Shui Tips for the Home*. St. Paul, MN: Llewellyn Publications, 1998.

———. *Amulets & Talismans for Beginners*. St. Paul, MN: Llewellyn Publications, 2004.

———. *The Encyclopedia of Superstitions*. Woodbury, MN: Llewellyn Publications, 2008.

———. *Feng Shui for Beginners*. St. Paul, MN: Llewellyn Publications, 1997.

———. *Feng Shui for Love and Romance*. St. Paul, MN: Llewellyn Publications, 1999.

———. *Write Your Own Magic*. St. Paul, MN: Llewellyn Publications, 2001.

Weinstein, Michael. *The World of Jewel Stones*. London: Sir Isaac Pitman and Son, 1959.

Wilson, John Albert. *The Culture of Ancient Egypt*. Chicago: University of Chicago Press, 1956.

Wiseman, Dr. Richard. *The Luck Factor: Change Your Luck—and Change Your Life*. London: Century Books, 2002.

Notes

Introduction

1. E. M. Forster, *The Longest Journey* (Edinburgh and London: William Blackwood and Sons, 1907), 212.

2. Max Gunther, *Instant Millionaires: The Secrets of Overnight Success* (Petersfield, UK: Harriman House Ltd., 2011; originally published 1973), 195.

3. Lysann Damisch, http://www.psychologicalscience.org/index .php/news/releases/keep-your-fingers-crossed -how-superstition-improves-performance.html

4. Eric Wargo, "The Many Lives of Superstition," in *Observer*, October 2008. Available online at: http://www .psychologicalscience.org/index.php/publications /observer/2008/october-08/the-many-lives-of-superstition .html.

Chapter One

1. Michael Neill, *The Inside Out Revolution* (Carlsbad, CA: Hay House, Inc., 2013), 23.

2. Sharon Begley, *Train Your Mind, Change Your Brain: How a New Science Reveals our Extraordinary Potential to Transform Ourselves* (New York: Ballantine Books, 2007), 90–92, 110–111.

3. David Shenk, *The Genius in All of Us: Why Everything You've Been Told About Genetics, Talent, and IQ is Wrong* (New York: Doubleday, 2010), 74–78.

4. Eleanor A. Maguire, Katherine Woollett, and Hugo J. Spiers, "London Taxi Drivers and Bus Drivers: A Structural MRI and Neuropsychological Analysis" (*Hippocampus* 16, 2006), 1091–1101. http://www.fil.ion.ucl.ac.uk/Maguire/Maguire2006.pdf See also: *The Knowledge*, Public Carriage Office, Transport for London. http://www.tfl.gov.uk/businessandpartners/taxisandprivatehire/1412.aspx.

5. "The Brain: How the Brain Rewires Itself." Article in *Time Magazine*, January 19, 2007. Available online at: http://www.time.com/time/magazine/article/0,9171,1580438-1,00.html.

Chapter Two

1. http://www.synergysuccessstrategies.com.au/admin/editor/uploaded/Metropolitan%20Life%20Case%20Study.pdf.

2. Steve Kilgallon, "What I Do," in Sunday supplement of *Star-Times*, New Zealand, July 22, 2012, 34.

3. Royston M. Roberts, *Serendipity: Accidental Discoveries in Science* (New York: John Wiley & Sons, Inc., 1989), 1–3.

4. http://www.healthassociatesllc.com/files/1352751786.pdf. Further information can be found in Dr. Seligman's books: *Authentic Happiness: Using the New Positive Psychology to Realize Your Potential for Lasting Fulfillment* (New York: Free Press, 2002) and *Learned Optimism: How to Change Your Mind and Your Life* (New York: Free Press, 1994).

5. Robert Emmons's books include: *The Psychology of Gratitude* (New York: Oxford University Press, 2004) and *Thanks! How the New Science of Gratitude Can Make You Happier* (Boston: Houghton-Mifflin Company, 2007).

6. *http://www.iamthankful.com/science/gratitude-interventions -project-by-dr-robert-emmons.*

7. Walter Winchell attributed the quote to J. J. Lerner in 1949, more than ten years before it was used by Gary Player. http ://quoteinvestigator.com/2010/07/14/luck/

8. Russell H. Conwell, *Acres of Diamonds* (Philadelphia: John Y. Huber Company, 1890).

9. Max Weber, translated by A. M. Henderson and Talcott Parsons, *The Theory of Social and Economic Organization* (New York: Oxford University Press, 1947), 328. See also: *On Charisma and Institution Building* by Max Weber, edited by S. N. Eisenstadt (Chicago: University of Chicago Press, 1968).

10. John Albert Wilson, *The Culture of Ancient Egypt* (Chicago: University of Chicago Press, 1956), 121.

Chapter Three

1. Richard Webster, *Write Your Own Magic* (St. Paul, MN: Llewellyn Publications, 2001), 125.

2. Ahmad ibn 'Ali al-Buni, quoted in *Credulities Past and Present* by William Jones (London: Chatto & Windus, 1880), 240.

Chapter Four

1. George Frederick Kunz, *The Curious Lore of Precious Stones* (Philadelphia: J. B. Lippincott Company, 1913), 307.

Chapter Five

1. Lysann Damisch, Barbara Stoberock, and Thomas Mussweiler, "Keep Your Fingers Crossed! How Superstition Improves Performance." Article in *Psychological Science*, May 27, 2010. Available online at: http://pss.sagepub.com/content/early/2010/05/27/0956797610372631.

2. Deborah Aaronson and Kevin Kwan, *Luck: The Essential Guide* (New York: HarperCollins, 2008), 11.

3. Leo Vinci, *Talismans, Amulets and Charms* (London: Regency Press, 1977), 45.

4. *The Holy Bible, King James Version* (Nashville, TN: Thomas Nelson Publishers), 1984.

5. E. A. Wallis Budge, *Amulets and Superstitions* (London: Oxford University Press, 1930), 490.

6. Richard Webster, *Omens, Oghams, and Oracles* (St. Paul, MN: Llewellyn Publications, 1995), 22–23.

7. Michael Weinstein, *The World of Jewel Stones* (London: Sir Isaac Pitman and Son, 1959), 71.

8. Carol Andrews, *Amulets of Ancient Egypt* (London: British Museum Press, 1994), 50.

9. E. A. Wallis Budge, *Amulets and Superstitions* (London: Oxford University Press, 1930), 134.

Chapter Seven

1. Richard Webster, *101 Feng Shui Tips for the Home* (St. Paul, MN: Llewellyn Publications, 1998), 2–3.

2. E. and M.A. Radford, (edited and revised by Christina Hole), *Encyclopaedia of Superstitions* (London: Hutchinson & Company [Publishers] Limited, 1961. Originally published in 1948), 333.

Chapter Ten

1. *Encyclopaedia Britannica, Macropaedia*, vol. 16, 15th ed. (Chicago: Encyclopaedia Britannica, Inc., 1983), 193.

Chapter Twelve

1. http://www.totalprosports.com/2012/10/17/justin-verlander -rub-detroit-tigers-trainer-bald-head-good-luck-video/.

2. Richard Webster, *Encyclopedia of Superstitions* (Woodbury, MN: Llewellyn Publications, 2008), 45.

3. http://collections.vam.ac.uk/item/O3311/the-luck-of -edenhall-beaker-and-case-unknown/.

Chapter Thirteen

1. http://www.time.com/time/politics/whitehouse
   /photos/0.27424.1811278.00.html.

2. Richard Wiseman and Caroline Watt, *Measuring Superstitious
   Belief: Why Lucky Charms Matter*, http://www.good-luck-gifts
   .com/presents/images/stories/Documents/Lucky_charms
   matter-_Wiseman.pdf.

3. David Derbyshire, "Lucky Charms DO Work: Study Proves
   They Increase Chance of Success," in *Daily Mail*, UK,
   July 15, 2010. http://www.dailymail.co.uk/sciencetech/
   article-1294985/Lucky-charms-DO-work-Study-proves
   -increase-chances-success.html.

4. Abraham Pais, *Inward Bound: Of Matters and Forces in the
   Physical World* (New York: Oxford University Press, 1986), 210.

To Write to the Author

If you wish to contact the author or would like more information about this book, please write to the author in care of Llewellyn Worldwide Ltd. and we will forward your request. Both the author and publisher appreciate hearing from you and learning of your enjoyment of this book and how it has helped you. Llewellyn Worldwide Ltd. cannot guarantee that every letter written to the author can be answered, but all will be forwarded. Please write to:

Richard Webster
℅ Llewellyn Worldwide
2143 Wooddale Drive
Woodbury, MN 55125-2989

Please enclose a self-addressed stamped envelope for reply,
or $1.00 to cover costs. If outside the U.S.A., enclose
an international postal reply coupon.

Many of Llewellyn's authors have websites with additional information and resources. For more information, please visit our website at http://www .llewellyn.com.